This Old House® complete landscaping

This Old House Books

New York

THIS OLD HOUSE BOOKS
IN CONJUNCTION WITH SUNSET BOOKS

FOR THIS OLD HOUSE:

Editorial Director: Paul Spring
President, This Old House Ventures: Eric Thorkilsen
Technical Consultants: Master Carpenter Norm Abram,
Landscape Contractor Roger Cook,
and General Contractor Tom Silva

FOR SUNSET BOOKS:

Vice President and General Manager: Richard A. Smeby
Vice President and Editorial Director: Bob Doyle
Production Director: Lory Day
Operations Director: Rosann Sutherland
Retail Sales Development Manager: Linda Barker

Managing Editor: Bridget Biscotti Bradley
Project Editor: Michael MacCaskey
Project and Photo Editor: Lynn Ocone
Art Director: Amy Gonzalez
Writers: Gary Keim, T. Jeff Williams
Additional Writers: Kathie Bond Borie,
Tim Thoelecke of Garden Concepts, Inc., Joseph Truini
Additional Technical Consultants:
Tom Bressan of The Urban Farmer Store,
Gary J. Kling, Dianne Noland
Consulting Editor: Margaret McKinnon
Illustrator: Troy Doolittle, TopDog Illustration
Copy Editor: Carol Whiteley
Page Production: Linda Bouchard
Photo Research: Kara Buchanan, Robert Hardin, Audrey Mak
Prepress Coordinator: Eligio Hernandez
Proofreader: John Edmonds
Indexer: Mary Pelletier-Hunyadi
Cover: Photography by Roger Foley; Richard Arentz,
Landscape Architect

For additional copies of *This Old House Complete Landscaping* call
Sunset Books at 1-800-526-5111 or visit us at www.sunset.com.

contents

LETTER
from This Old House

MOST OF US THINK OF OUR FRONT AND BACK yards as an extension of our home. But there's a difference—a big difference—between inside and out. Inside, walls don't bloom, chandeliers don't change color and drop their leaves, and carpeting doesn't need to be mowed weekly.

The fact that your landscaping will continue to grow and change is why planning makes such a difference in whether it works for you and your family, and how easy it is to maintain. This applies to everything from hardscaping—patios, paths, benches, hot tubs, arbors, and decks—to trees and shrubs, perennials and cutting gardens. They'll all come together to create an oasis that will become even more beautiful and enjoyable each year if you follow the simple guidelines and advice offered in the pages that follow.

Enjoy the time outside, whether you're working on the yard or just giving the hammock a workout.

Roger Cook

This Old House Landscape Contractor

planning

WITH A PLAN AND SOME KNOW-HOW, YOU CAN CREATE
AN OUTDOOR LIVING SPACE FOR YEAR-ROUND ENJOYMENT

CREATING AN ATTRACTIVE AND PRACTICAL LANDSCAPE
is a deeply satisfying accomplishment. But where
do you begin? And what parts should you tackle
yourself? The truth is that many paths can lead
to a successful outcome if you have the right
information on the steps involved. This chapter
gets you started, whether you're undertaking an
overgrown landscape or a completely barren one.

As you begin to think seriously about landscaping
or relandscaping your garden, it will help greatly to
collect pictures and ideas from gardening books
and magazines. Also visit gardens in your area,
taking photographs as you go and noting which
plants look best in which season.

Once you have a good collection of ideas,
you are ready to take the plunge and begin your
landscape plan. As *This Old House* landscape
contractor Roger Cook notes, "You wouldn't build
a house without a well-thought-out plan, and you
shouldn't try to landscape without one, either."

Be realistic about your property's assets and
liabilities, and what is possible given the topography
and your budget. Decide which features to keep and
which you want to change. Remember, it's best to
make these decisions once you've lived on the
property for at least a year so you know how it
looks and how you use it in all seasons.

landscaping step by step

It is rewarding and relatively easy to conjure the landscape of your dreams, but before the vision can become reality, it's important to understand what the overall process involves.

Knowing the correct sequence of tasks means you won't have to undo something you thought was finished, or realize you've missed the right stage for taking an important step. Before work begins is also the time to make choices, such as which parts of the project to do yourself and when to consult a professional.

Make a plan, get permits
Whether you develop it yourself or already have one, you'll need a plot plan showing the existing features of your house, landscape, and property lines. The plan will become the basis for your base plan (see page 18). If you're lucky, a plot plan accompanies the deed to your house. Otherwise, check with your city or county building or planning department, which can also tell you of any zoning, code, and building ordinances that could affect your proposed plans. Among the considerations are property boundaries, easements, and setback and lot-coverage requirements. Once you have a base plan, you can develop your landscape design and plans for installing it.

A small loader makes quick work of demolition.

Before any work begins, make sure you have obtained all required permits, located underground utilities, decided on materials and plants (and checked on their availability), signed up with any contractors you'll need later on, reserved any necessary rental tools, and arranged for trash disposal.

Prepare the site Begin by removing trees, shrubs, lawns, and any other unwanted elements, and disposing of debris. Leave only plants and features that will be part of the new landscape; mark and protect them. You may need to fence off the project's perimeter as well as trees and shrubs that you want to keep (see pages

68–69), and perhaps define an access route for heavy equipment and delivery of materials.

Establish a rough grade This step is necessary to determine the final soil level and to ensure that surface water flows away from the house. While rough grading you can create berms and contours that direct water drainage, create privacy, and make the landscape more interesting. Rough grading also includes setting aside topsoil to spread before final planting, and removing excess soil from one area to fill in elsewhere.

If your yard is on a hillside, or if you have to manage water movement around (or through) your yard, this is a good time to enlist the help of a civil engineer or experienced landscape professional. Likewise, moving large amounts of soil is usually a job for a contractor with heavy equipment.

Lay out utility lines This includes laying electrical conduit (if necessary for lights and controllers; low-voltage lines require no conduit), gas lines, and water lines. If you don't know exactly what will be needed, which is often the case, install large-diameter chase or sleeve pipes underneath potential obstacles so you won't have to dig up or under that new pathway. While the locations of these lines may seem obvious and easy to remember now, they may not be later. Be sure to mark their locations on your plan.

Also establish the placement of features that will be put in later, such as a pool or pond, and note walks, paths, patios, and play areas.

Complete construction Now's the time to complete any projects that involve heavy equipment, whether for structures or for planting large boxed trees. This is a labor-intensive stage; consider using a contractor for specialized work.

Finish grading and irrigation Once all construction projects are completed, get the soil ready for planting. Spread topsoil saved from the grading stage onto planting beds or lawn areas; also add any amendments or fertilizers needed. Install sprinklers for the lawn and adjust as needed. If the system has an electronic controller, make sure it works before filling trenches. Then establish the final grade and finish installing sprinklers and landscape lighting systems.

Plant This satisfying phase of actually putting most of the plants into the ground comes last to protect them from the rigors of construction. Start with the largest plants (not including the box-size trees that went in earlier), moving on to smaller shrubs, ground

covers, and perennials. Order plants for delivery as close to planting day as possible and inspect them on arrival for quality and health. Once planting of shrubs and ground covers is complete, finish up with sprinklers or drip systems as needed. Then, finally, when everything else is done, plant the lawn.

One artful aspect of landscaping is timing all the preliminary work so that the plants go into the ground at the most favorable time. When everything is in place, sweep, clean up debris, adjust sprinklers if needed, and enhance the new landscape with some mulch. Then find a comfortable seat and enjoy the fruits of your labor.

At the end of the project, sprinkler heads get a final adjustment to ensure they're covering intended areas.

Almost anyone can handle finish grading and planting, but other steps require a bit more expertise. When it comes to figuring out who is going to do the heavy lifting, Roger Cook's rule of thumb is "If the project is going to take you more than two weekends, consider hiring a pro."

LANDSCAPE DESIGNERS know the plants that do well locally, and they are familiar with local landscaping resources. Most are willing to work on small projects, and they charge fees ranging from $40 to $100 an hour.

LANDSCAPE ARCHITECTS have studied design at a university and are state licensed to design more complex grading, retaining walls, and drainage systems. Their fees start at $100 an hour.

LANDSCAPE CONTRACTORS are installation specialists, often working closely with designers or architects. Their fees range from $40 to $80 an hour.

When it comes to choosing plants, garden-center pros can suggest options. Or check with your county's cooperative extension office. There you'll find state university landscape specialists who are generally well informed about which plants work best in your area.

beginning to plan

Review all the features around your house. What looks good and what needs to change? How well do different parts of the property work together, both functionally and aesthetically?

How does your front yard look to passersby? You don't have to be satisfied with the standard-issue front yard: a patch of lawn, foundation plantings, a tree or two, and an unclear or uninviting route to the front door. Often a few minor adjustments make a more attractive look. Simply updating the entry by making it wider or easier to navigate pays substantial dividends. A simple pot of flowers by the front door reinforces your welcome to guests, as does a bed of annuals and perennials.

Does the landscape reflect your taste and needs as well as the style of your house? There's plenty of room for creativity and many styles that might work for your home. Learning about your house's history and style is likely to prompt a variety of inspirations for your project, especially if you can find old photos.

For even more inspiration, look to other homes in your neighborhood and local public gardens. Keep a notepad handy and write down which entryways you like, what are the best plantings, and so forth. It sounds simple, but this is one of the most practical ways to pick up useful ideas.

Year-round good looks and easy outdoor entertaining were the design intentions here. For more details on this garden, see pages 18 through 23. Design: Richard Arentz

FEATURES OF A WELL-DESIGNED LANDSCAPE

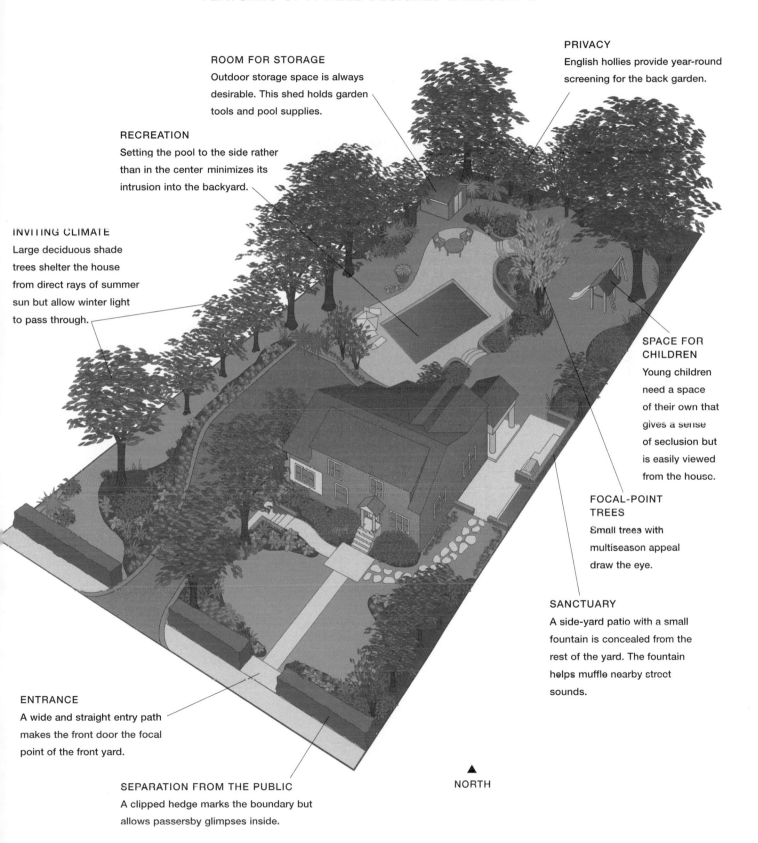

ROOM FOR STORAGE
Outdoor storage space is always desirable. This shed holds garden tools and pool supplies.

PRIVACY
English hollies provide year-round screening for the back garden.

RECREATION
Setting the pool to the side rather than in the center minimizes its intrusion into the backyard.

INVITING CLIMATE
Large deciduous shade trees shelter the house from direct rays of summer sun but allow winter light to pass through.

SPACE FOR CHILDREN
Young children need a space of their own that gives a sense of seclusion but is easily viewed from the house.

FOCAL-POINT TREES
Small trees with multiseason appeal draw the eye.

SANCTUARY
A side-yard patio with a small fountain is concealed from the rest of the yard. The fountain helps muffle nearby street sounds.

ENTRANCE
A wide and straight entry path makes the front door the focal point of the front yard.

SEPARATION FROM THE PUBLIC
A clipped hedge marks the boundary but allows passersby glimpses inside.

▲
NORTH

landscape styles

Consider various landscape styles as they relate to your taste, surroundings, and lifestyle. You may prefer the calm order of a formal symmetrical garden with close-cropped hedges, or the cacophony of one that emulates nature and allows plants to have their own shapes. Of course, a successful garden needn't be all one style; it could be quite manicured near the house and more natural toward the perimeter.

Pay attention to your house's style and materials and any natural features on your property or nearby. Around a colonial-style house, a landscape of cactus and other desert plants would be out of place, as would a formal garden in front of a Southwestern adobe.

Red wicker chairs add shots of color to an already bright tangle of hollyhocks, coneflowers, and daisies in this casual garden.

If you have children and pets, you'll have to think about the spaces they'll need. But if your garden will be a one- or two-person retreat from hectic workdays, you can focus on the quiet and privacy you need.

Are you a cook, artist, or plant lover? You may want to create a garden around favorite herbs and unusual plants.

This Mediterranean-style, low-maintenance dry garden complements a Spanish-style house. Plants include gray lavender cotton (Santolina) and lavender.

A formal hedge of sheared Japanese boxwood (Buxus) is softened by spring-blooming daffodils interplanted with blue forget-me-nots (Myosotis).

high-profile bloomers need regular watering, pruning, and fertilizing, and lawns require more frequent attention than almost any other part of the garden. However, shrubs and many perennials are good low-maintenance choices and offer year-round structure and beauty.

Think of your area's natural environment. Even if you're surrounded by built-up streetscape, it's likely that native plants can fit in beautifully. Such plants are usually better adapted to local rainfall and seasonal temperatures than imported plants are, and less likely to become invasive. They're also generally less susceptible to pests and diseases.

As your plan evolves, be realistic. Who will maintain the garden? Even if you enjoy gardening, limited time can be a constraint. Roses and other

ABOVE: Big-leaved Dutchman's pipe (Aristolochia) on the lattice and elephant's ears (Alocasia) in the pots give a lush feel to a traditional pool setting.
LEFT: The informality of a kidney-shaped pool and free-flowering perennials in curving beds creates a softer look.

landscape design basics

No matter what style you choose for your landscape, the resulting design should be governed by some basic principles that complement each other. When correctly applied, these principles—unity, balance, transition, proportion or scale, rhythm, views and focal points, and order (repetition and simplicity)—ensure a garden that's pleasing to look at and be in.

A straight grassy path lined with perennials and sheared hedges creates a visual guide for visitors.

An asymmetrical curving path of red and buff flagstone seems more familiar with clumps of grass and boulders bedded along opposite edges.

■ *Unity* gives a garden consistency. All the parts look as if they were meant to be together, and no one plant, structure, or feature dominates, unless it's intended as a focal point.

■ *Balance* can be achieved through symmetry in a formal garden (features on one side of an axis are mirror images of those on the other side) or by asymmetry (different features provide balance on each side of an axis, such as a path).

■ *Transition* is handled with elements arranged in logical order so that the viewer's eye is drawn along. The draw might be a distant view outside the actual garden, or it could be changing textures, forms, and sizes of leaves and plants along a path.

■ *Proportion* is how the sizes of the various elements of the design relate to each other. Ideally, no element—tree, shrub, pathway, or fence—seems too large or too small compared with others. Well-planned, simple spaces are restful, with just the right balance of close-up and more distant detail.

■ *Rhythm* is created from a sense of motion as the viewer is led along, seeing various parts of the garden in sequence. To make the design change and move, elements such as paving or wall surfaces can be repeated, alternated, or inverted, or be used in different sizes or colors.

■ *Views and focal points* direct the eye to different distances and draw people through the garden. The best view may even be beyond the garden itself, or it could be from the house into the garden. A focal point can be a magnificent saucer magnolia, a pond, a beautiful pot, or a statue.

■ *Order* is established through the overall framework of the design, as well as through its parts, such as trees and built structures. These are often aligned along a central axis such as a view or walk.

From an inviting swing, the pond and distant view are restful focal points.

other considerations

Besides the basics, consider the colors you prefer—hot yellows or reds, or cool blues and greens. Placing opposite colors, such as red and green or orange and blue, adjacent to each other creates excitement. On the other hand, colors that are similar, such as orange and yellow, create a soothing feel. Also use color to focus attention: warm colors appear closer, while cool colors recede.

Color comes from more than flowers. Consider plants' bark, berries, and fruits. Landscape designers also consider form, line, and texture. Form relates to a plant's three-dimensional shape: tall and slender or short and squat. Line refers to the visual patterns on two dimensions. They may be geometric, as in formal gardens, or curving, as in most modern home landscapes. Texture relates primarily to the size or feel of a plant or object. Small leaves have a fine texture, as do those that are soft to the touch. Bold, large-leaved plants have a coarse texture.

Contrasting textures of false cypress (Chamaecyparis), barberry (Berberis), and spiraea create interest in a garden around a pond.

soil and microclimates

Take a good look at your immediate surroundings, including the terrain and soil. Along with your area's climate and your property's microclimates, these are the basic factors you will work with, and they influence what you can plant. The factors are described below. Rank them in order of their importance to you, and use the results to guide your planning. Zoning and building ordinances also come into play here; check with your building department before you launch into a design.

terrain and soil

Collect information and details about lot size, slope, sun exposure, and soil characteristics. Is the lot large enough for all the activities you'd like to include—entertaining, games, children's play? If not, where can you compromise? A slope, either above or below your house, can add interest, but it may need to be terraced or otherwise modified to be safe and, perhaps, usable.

Early in the planning process, have a soil test done; for sources, check with a county or state cooperative extension office. Soil may be too acid or alkaline or contain harmful salts. It may drain poorly or have a layer of hardpan underneath. Adding organic matter such as compost,

Living umbrellas, low and wide-spreading fruitless mulberry trees (Morus alba), *make dense shade all summer but allow the sun's rays to reach the patio in winter.*

well-rotted manure, or soil amendments before planting improves most soils. Also use soil conditioners such as sulfur or lime to correct acidity or alkalinity.

climate and microclimates

The weather conditions in your area, averaged over years, primarily determines what you can plant, how much time you can spend outdoors during the year, and how much water is generally available.

Consider the assets—and the liabilities—of your area's climate. If it's mild year-round, plan to make the

outdoors as livable as possible, with spaces to relax, cook, and play. On the other hand, if the outdoor season is very short, think of ways to make the most of your outdoor time, concentrating on the activities that are most important to you.

Sun and wind exposure, low-lying pockets that trap cold air, overhanging eaves, and tree windbreaks or fencing can influence or even create microclimates. The challenge is to recognize them, then work with or modify them when you design your landscape, position a patio or deck, or decide what to plant (see lower illustration, opposite page).

For instance, slopes that drop to the south or southwest get more daytime heat than those that drop to the north or northeast. Similarly, walls running east to west reflect extra heat and sunlight onto plants on their south sides. North-south walls reflect extra heat onto plants on their west sides but create cooler microclimates on their east sides. Sunny locations are best for heat-loving plants, but the soil dries out faster and requires extra irrigation.

The effects of seasonal climate changes are more subtle. During summer, the sun is higher in the sky and days are longer, meaning only those areas immediately beside the house

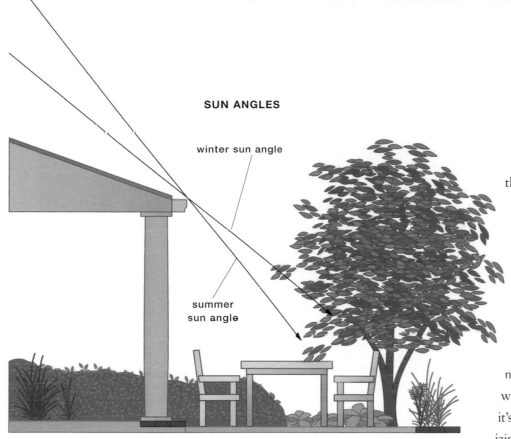

SUN ANGLES

winter sun angle

summer
sun angle

are shaded. In winter, the sun is low in the southern sky, so north-facing exposures receive much less sun. These effects become more pronounced at northern latitudes but are important factors to consider throughout North America.

A patio in full summer sun will need sun-tempering measures, while a patio that receives low winter sun will be warmed, a bonus during cold months. If you don't consider these factors carefully, your outdoor spaces may not be as inviting as you'd hoped they would be.

legal considerations

Your city or county building department's building codes regulate what a given landscaping project can or must include.

For example, what are your lot's setbacks, and are there restrictions on what can be built in those areas? How high can fencing be? How must outbuildings be positioned? Often, permanent structures are prohibited on city easements, and fence heights are typically limited to 6 feet. Does

the lot contain heritage trees that must be saved, or is it infested with weeds, brush, and nuisance plants that must be removed?

Also keep in mind—for good community relations as well as legal reasons—how the changes you're contemplating will affect neighbors. Even if neighbors don't have to be notified when the permitting process starts, it's smart to talk to them before finalizing plans. Don't be dismayed; you might pick up some additional ideas.

The preceding is, in a nutshell, the way to get started planning your new landscape. The remainder of this chapter takes you through the next steps of planning, closing with several examples of successfully renovated landscapes to inspire you.

COLD-AIR POCKETS

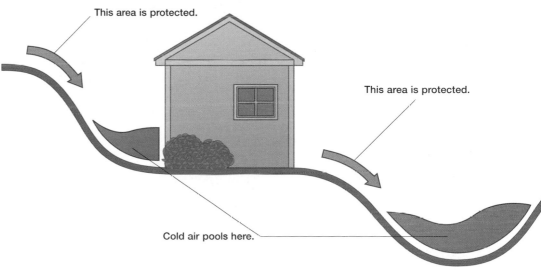

This area is protected.

This area is protected.

Cold air pools here.

develop a base plan

Before you can turn your wishes and ideas into a coherent and aesthetically pleasing final plan, you'll need to work on a scale diagram of your property, or plot plan. This diagram will become your base plan and, finally, your new landscape plan.

If you're lucky, you may find a deed map that gives the property's dimensions and orientation; the next best thing is a topographical plan. Also check with your town or county property or land department for such maps; architectural plans depict sites as well. If nothing is available, you can measure the lot's features and transfer them to graph paper; a good scale is ¼ inch to 1 foot.

If the terrain is complicated or the lot irregular, consider hiring a professional surveyor, engineer, or landscape designer. If you're doing it yourself, use a 100-foot steel tape and enlist a helper. Be prepared to measure everything on your lot: perimeter boundaries and dimensions; topography (high and low points), drainage, and exposure; placement and size of buildings, with windows, doors, eaves,

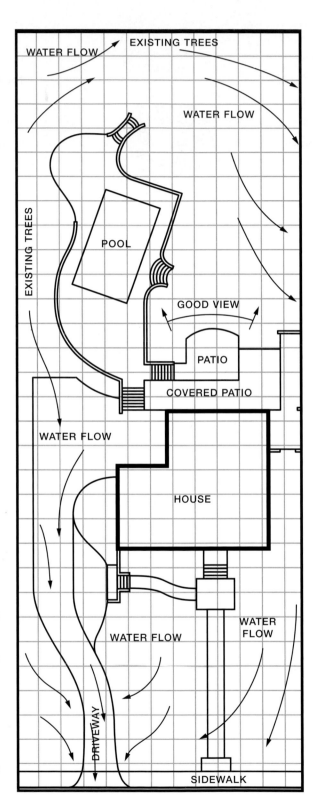

downspouts, and drains marked; location of decks, patios, paths, fences, and so on; utility lines, easements, and setbacks; location of existing plants, lawn, shrubs, and large trees; soil conditions, including filled or badly draining areas; direction of prevailing winds; and any other relevant information. If views are important or unsightly intrusions need to be hidden, mark their direction.

Make the base plan as accurate as possible, including as many details as you can. Then, just to be safe, make working copies. Place one copy under a sheet of tracing paper to begin your bubble plan and, ultimately, your final plan.

bubble diagrams

The bubble diagram is usually little more than a doodle, but it is a good way to get started thinking on paper. Think in terms of spaces and their functions rather than in details or precise shapes.

This is the time to be fanciful; if an idea clearly doesn't work, just move on to another piece of paper.

BUBBLE DIAGRAM

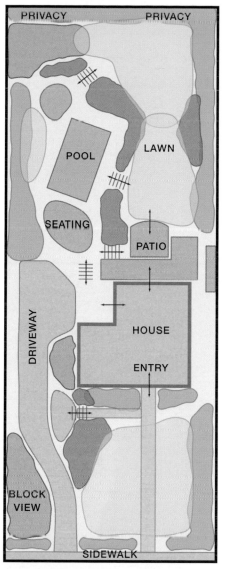

To make a bubble diagram, place tracing paper over your base plan, then sketch in rough circles, squares, or triangles to indicate different activities and garden areas you want to incorporate (right). Where areas share more than one activity, let the bubbles overlap. Also note areas that need screening from sun, neighbors, or wind.

As you sketch, think of different areas and how they will be used. For example, play areas for small children should be within view of wherever an adult is most likely to be, and trash and garden tools should be out of the way yet accessible. Choose the best locations for patios, decks, and storage.

Keep in mind how much space each activity or setting requires.

(The diagrams below give specifics for path and bench clearance.) This information will help you critique your first passes at a bubble diagram. Perhaps the patio you drew is really too large for the available space. Maybe garden structures or activity areas intrude too much into quieter locales. Don't let these issues stop you now; just keep sketching until you're satisfied.

Look closely to see what works and what doesn't in terms of your preferences. Put down another layer of tracing paper and take another pass, then look again. Compare the pros and cons of the different bubble diagrams. If you keep at it, you will find yourself getting closer to a final version of your plan.

PATHWAY CLEARANCE

SERVICE PATHWAY 2' TO 3'

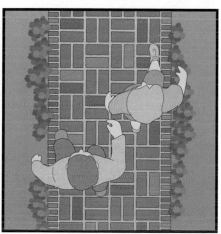

MAIN PATHWAY 4' TO 5'

BENCH CLEARANCE

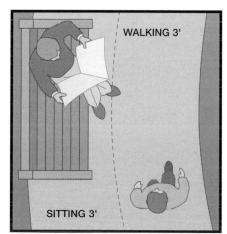

choosing plants

The last step in planning is choosing plants. But before you get down to specifics, think of the types of plants you need based on functions: evergreens for all-year screening, a deciduous tree to maximize winter sunlight, a 10-foot-tall shrub to anchor a border, or a vine to climb over a trellis or fence.

The shape of your property may dictate certain types of plants. For instance, a low, deep-rooted ground cover may be the answer for a slope on which a lawn just wouldn't work.

Once you know the type of plant you need, your selection is significantly narrowed, which helps make choices easier.

Some landscape maintenance is inevitable, but you can minimize it. Choose plants according to their mature size, or the size at which you can easily (and willingly) maintain them. And use only plants that are well adapted to their location and

A deciduous tree at the corner serves as a visual anchor and frames the entry. Low foundation plantings sweep toward the entry in a broad curve, also serving to guide the focus. Container plantings at the entrance soften the transition from paving to landscape.

These entry plantings are mostly long-lived shrubs, providing color with minimal maintenance.

environment. No matter how well a plant fits in the space or how beautiful its flowers, if it struggles to grow for lack of water, light, or the right soil, it will be less attractive, if not a maintenance problem. By the same token, avoid invasive or pest-prone plants. Plants that grow well without much help look best.

Keep your landscape plan simple. Simplicity is the key to both lower maintenance and effective results. Use a small number of plants with different characteristics and repeat them. Use even fewer unusual plants. Create simple lines for edges of borders, walks, and drives. And use simple arrangements for groupings of plants.

Shape your planting beds to have either straight or gradually curving lines. This makes maintenance easier and helps direct the viewer's eye. Avoid sudden dips and jags, and orient bed lines at right angles where they meet a sidewalk or structure to give a sense of completion. For help with plant selection, see Chapter 5, beginning on page 138, and consider taking your plan to a garden center.

HOW A DESIGNER SEES PLANTS

SPECIMEN PLANTS attract attention and deserve a prominent place in the landscape, but they should be used sparingly to make them stand out.

ACCENT PLANTS differ from the plants around them, but the contrast is more subtle than with specimen plants.

CORNER PLANTS are used at the corners of the house to blend the vertical line of the walls with the horizontal plane of the ground.

FOUNDATION PLANTS, like corner plantings, connect the house with the ground. These plantings should direct the eye to the entrance, not camouflage it.

ENTRANCE PLANTS identify and direct visitors to the entrance. To welcome visitors, groupings of plants, such as a collection of colorful container plants, work well near the front door.

BORDER PLANTS divide and define spaces in the yard. A border may be low or tall, but it is usually taller at the back and center and lower toward the front and ends.

SCREEN PLANTS are groupings of plants (usually at least 6 feet tall) that hide or cover unwanted views or objects. Evergreen plants make effective screens.

the final plan

Once you've created a bubble diagram that incorporates your ideas, go back to the base plan. Using overlays, begin fitting the new spaces onto it until you come up with a functional, aesthetically pleasing design.

If you want to customize landscape elements, you can design your own fence, deck railings, trellises, paving patterns, and other details rather than buy them "off the rack."

Keep revising until the plan works; paper is cheap. As Roger Cook says, "It's easy to move a tree or walkway on paper, but it's not once it's installed. If you invest time up front to create a plan you're happy with and will stick to, you'll save money in the end."

ABOVE: Wall and steps merge with blue-stone patio and irregular edge at lawn.
RIGHT: A porch and open patio are perfect for entertaining and the main platform for viewing the landscape.

This narrow side-yard strip, visible year-round from the kitchen, is transformed by a pond and paving into a separate, quiet space.

Then you're off to the races. Set up a schedule that allows time for planning, building, and planting. If possible, spread the work out so that planting can be done at the best time for your area, preferably fall in mild-winter climates or spring elsewhere. This way, the plants will get a good start.

THE FINAL PLAN

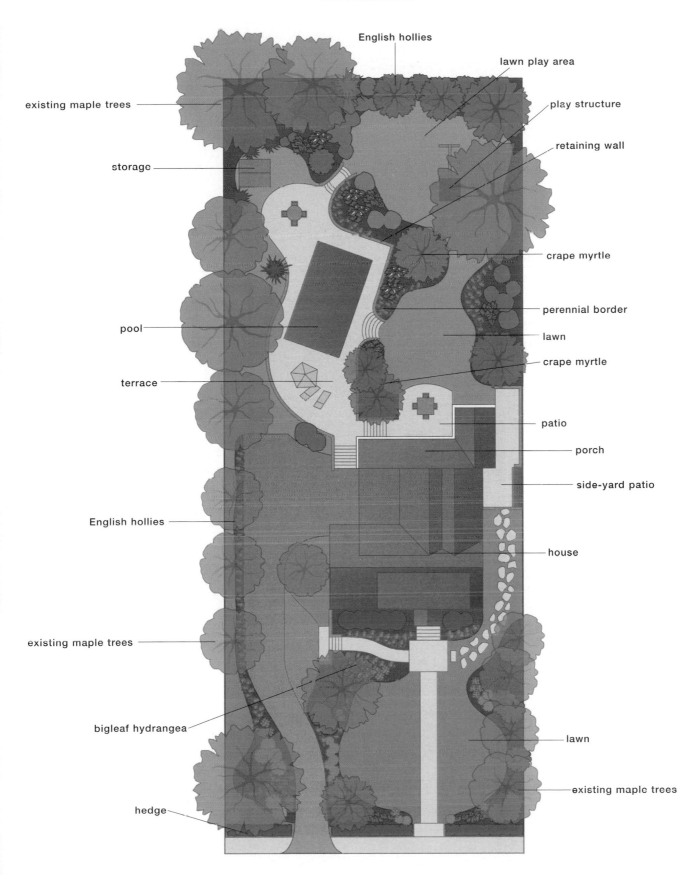

English hollies

lawn play area

play structure

retaining wall

existing maple trees

storage

crape myrtle

perennial border

pool

lawn

crape myrtle

terrace

patio

porch

side-yard patio

English hollies

house

existing maple trees

lawn

bigleaf hydrangea

existing maple trees

hedge

before and after

BEFORE: Weed-choked lawn, concrete patio, and glaring white house and roof were a turnoff for outdoor activities.
AFTER: Brick-banded charcoal-colored flagstone paves the patio outside the living room, kitchen, and master bedroom. Fifteen-light French doors replaced tired aluminum-framed units.

The following pages contain relandscaping ideas from four houses typical in many parts of the country: ranch-style homes in Texas and Southern California, a tract house in Arizona, and a Cape Cod house in Massachusetts. Their landscapes have grown and evolved over the years to become inviting havens for outdoor living.

combining areas

In the improve-don't-move school, the owners of this one-story ranch in Houston stand out as veterans. When they bought the house nearly 20 years ago, a chain-link fence separated their weed-choked lawn and pea-gravel patio from their neighbors' grounds. Their first makeover included a wooden deck, an arbor, and a hot tub; they also sandblasted the old stucco walls of the house to reveal the brick underneath. But by the late 1990s, those amenities seemed out of date. With the help of landscape architects, the owners planned and executed a complete redesign.

Their scheme encompasses three interrelated areas. Closest to the house is a 20-square-foot patio, the part of the redesign the couple uses most. Paved in charcoal colored buckhorn flagstone and banded in brick, the patio is reached from the house through new doors. Because the flagstones were laid atop the old bed of pea gravel, the patio is elevated 6 inches above the adjoining graveled seating area. A 5-by-6-foot brick-walled fishpond (right) marks the junction between the raised, paved patio and the gravel area; the revamped pump that fed the old hot tub now circulates water in the pond.

A seating area bordered by trees and shrubs rests on the lawn below the patio. The steps start as single pieces of flagstone that frame the gravel, then meander in a free-form route through the grass to end at a 30-foot-long stone seat-wall (above). Wax-leaf privets (Ligustrum japonicum) and wood fencing screen the property from neighbors to the rear.

To complement the hardscape design, the plants are lush yet require little maintenance. On one patio wall a trellis of vinyl-coated cable supports thriving star jasmine (Trachelospermum jasminoides); below, maidenhair fern (Adiantum) and leopard plant (Ligularia tussilaginea 'Aureo-maculata') offset the flagstones. Shooting star (Dodecatheon primulaceae) and crape myrtle (Lagerstroemia indica) flank the doors into the living room.

Together, the patio and lawn provide a versatile outdoor room for the owners to enjoy alone or with friends. Guests gravitate to the bench at the end of the yard, returning to the patio when dinner is served.

BEFORE: Bermuda grass, Italian cypress by the mailbox, and a bougainvillea clump by the front door could hardly be called landscaping. AFTER: A flagstone path curves past grasses, succulents, and a mesquite tree, all suited to the desert. Pebble mulch hides the irrigation system. Low walls and screen add interest.

desert oasis

In recent years, natural gardens have been gaining ground across the country. Homeowners are planting prairies along Wisconsin streets, native wildflowers in New England woodland gardens, coastal scrub in California gardens, and desert plants in Arizona subdivisions. They are restoring natural vegetation not only because they like watching butterflies and birds but because a landscape that supports wildlife rarely requires pesticides, fertilizers, or much water.

The relandscaping design for the Phoenix tract house shown above simply followed nature. Instead of a water-guzzling lawn and thirsty plants, there are plants suited to low rainfall (Phoenix gets only 7 to 8 inches a year, equally received from winter rain and summer thunderstorms) and extreme heat (summer temperatures often climb past 110°F).

Desert vegetation is adapted to this harsh climate. Some plants have leaves that are heat-reflecting gray or waxy, thick, and leathery. Others, including cacti, have no leaves; their green, water-hoarding stems make food by photosynthesis. Many flowers are annuals, spending the greater part of their lives as seeds and awaiting the rain that signals them to sprout, bloom, and set new seeds.

Buried drip-irrigation lines take moisture directly to the plants without surface evaporation. In a new landscape, drip irrigation gives new plants a faster start; later on, it can supplement water in extremely dry periods. A flow of fist-size river cobbles simulates a stream and serves as mulch, cutting down on surface evaporation and conserving water. The large rocks create microhabitats as well: perennials planted at the stones' east-facing bases receive good morning light but are protected from brutal heat later in the day.

ranch redux

This 1960s California stucco ranch house underwent a transformation inside and out, yet without tearing down a lot of walls. The result is not flashy or glamorous; it's understated and intriguing.

The renovation was spurred by the 1994 Northridge earthquake, which made crucial repairs to the house necessary. The design that took shape was driven by the owner's desire to create a place that was formal yet embracing, where she could entertain friends and family yet also feel perfectly happy by herself.

A new fountain in the front courtyard is a big key to the calm feeling of the house. The sound of the water sets the mood as soon as you walk in. And because people gravitate to the fountain, the out-door space is now a dynamic extension of the interior.

Adding a water line to refill the fountain was easy: the architect simply extended an existing irrigation system for two palm trees. He built the pond's form out of 6-inch-thick concrete block, stuccoed the interior wall and applied a waterproof coating, then stacked slate around the structure. The top layer of slate is sturdy enough to double as seating. At the bottom of the fountain, river rock conceals lights as well as the pump that recycles water up through a column to a custom-made copper basin divided into four squares. The water pools in the squares, then trickles over the edge. Custom fountains can be pricey. For a less expensive option, consider a simpler decorative basin.

BEFORE: Standard 1960 Los Angeles ranch showed its age. AFTER: Translucent double doors lead to a bright courtyard, complete with trickling fountain. Low-maintenance shrubs replace thirsty ones.

Street-side doors open through stuccoed block walls to a flagstone-paved court-yard. The walls create total privacy, and the fountain masks street noise.

BEFORE: This mound of topsoil will create contours and garden beds on an otherwise flat lot. AFTER: Differing heights and colors of miscanthus grass, chrysanthemums, and 'Montgomery' blue spruce add texture as well as color.

landscaping in stages

The Massachusetts landscape shown here started as a barren yard, but to its owners, a landscape designer and a horticulturist, it was a field of possibilities. Their master plan for the 2½-acre property transformed an uninteresting field into an inviting landscape. Because of the magnitude of the job, the owners broke it into three phases to be worked on over three years. The project started with a plan, as all landscapes should. But it was a flexible one. The owners make the point easily: "Dreams are cheap. Moving earth is expensive."

The first phase made some big changes to the dead-flat lot. To make the house seem bigger, the owners raised the grade over a 24-by-36-foot area in front of the house and enclosed it with a picket fence to create a distinct front yard. Next, they moved the long driveway that divided the property into two pieces and created a graceful, curving one along one side of the property, partially screening it from the house

BELOW: Creating the shade garden was a three-year process, beginning with soil preparation. RIGHT: Next, two dogwood trees were transplanted from elsewhere on the property, and finally came the shade-loving plants.

with sloping mounds, or berms. This required a bulldozer and 300 cubic yards of topsoil. But the berms give the land a variety of heights and forms, and more features to catch the eye.

The owners stress that improving drainage should be part of the first stage of any landscaping project: "Most plants don't like soggy soil, and dealing with the problem later means tearing up landscaping you've already installed." If grading isn't sufficient, underground drains may be necessary.

CHAPTER TWO

ideas

GET YOUR CREATIVE JUICES FLOWING BY COLLECTING IDEAS
FROM SOME OF OUR FAVORITE GARDENS

FOR LANDSCAPE PIZZAZZ, NOTHING BEATS ANNUAL OR perennial flowers or knockout flowering shrubs. But to set off these plants and give the garden shape and utility, you'll need structures such as a fence, deck, arbor, or path. As with a house, such structures are built with familiar materials— wood, masonry, and paint—but because they are outdoors, you must take into account the added complexities of year-round exposure to weather or contact with soil.

Garden structures also play various design roles. Fences and trellises can create separate "rooms" in a backyard, and low, wide walls can provide seating as well. Gazebos, arbors, and overheads add shelter, privacy, and support for plants, while spas, outdoor kitchens, and decks can re-create the ambience and convenience of indoor rooms. But structures are the costliest part of any garden, so plan them with care. Research a broad range of materials in order to choose those that best fit with your needs, taste, and budget. By making the right choices, you will also be able to connect your outdoor spaces to your home and its surrounding environment.

decks

These quintessential outdoor rooms not only add beauty and value to your home, they are also great solutions for sloping, bumpy, or poorly draining ground. A wooden deck—either freestanding or attached to the house—provides a solid, relatively durable surface requiring no more than yearly maintenance.

Consider a deck if your house is on a steep hillside or if the doorsill is more than a couple of feet above grade. Although stone, brick, and

When a spectacular view is part of your home site, plan a deck to take advantage of it.

concrete patios can be added to steep sites, it is usually very difficult and costly to build the structures needed to support such materials.

A low-lying deck can link house and garden at above-grade level, smoothing out bumps and riding over drainage swales that might preclude masonry paving. In contrast, a deck that is one or more steps above floor level can feel awkward and exposed.

Decks often allow you to add features not possible with patio alternatives, such as built-in seating and storage spaces (both built-in and

The hot tub, bar table, porch-style swing, and plants complement the wooded setting of this redwood deck.

below the deck). Or a deck can surround a hot tub or pool that would otherwise be above grade, minimizing the tub's intrusion into the area.

design

Plan your deck to be a transition from house to garden, to complement the architecture of the house, and to integrate with the landscape. Ways to tie the deck to the house include repeating an architectural detail from the house in the deck, adding built-in planter boxes, integrating a gazebo or screened porch, and building in benches or tables. The goal is to make the deck part of the whole landscape rather than something attached to the house as an afterthought.

If the deck will be the primary outdoor living space, consider how it will appear from neighboring properties. Without careful siting, it can easily end up functioning as a stage on which your outdoor life plays to the entire neighborhood. If you prefer privacy, consider decks that are built

Sunk 1½ inches below the deck's surface, the hot tub appears to float inside its 6-inch-wide redwood molding. The tub itself rests on a concrete slab.

on more than one level. An upper level adjacent to the house can serve as a transition to a more intimate space. If the elevation change is not too severe, the lower level could also be a brick or stone patio.

When designing your deck, start by thinking about how you will use it. For example, if entertaining is part of your lifestyle and you want to use the deck for large parties, then broad steps can double as extra seating.

A series of decks connected by steps and paths accommodates changes in elevation and helps divide the yard into smaller, distinct areas.

materials

Few materials can match wood's natural texture and quality. Wood is durable and resilient underfoot and won't store heat the way masonry materials do (though this can be an advantage where nights are cool). For lower maintenance and environmental impact, consider plastic composite decking that is made to look like wood, though you'll still need wood for strong posts and joists.

Treated lumber can survive outdoors for decades longer than untreated wood. For many years, the most widely available product was Southern pine treated with chromated copper arsenate (CCA). This preservative is effective but is being phased out because of concerns about its arsenic content. Several newer options are now available. Hem-fir treated with ammoniacal copper quaternary (ACQ) is available in many areas, as is Southern pine treated with copper azole (CA-B). Whatever type of preservative is used, always dispose of sawdust and debris; never burn scraps. When working with these materials, wear a dust mask, goggles, and gloves.

Untreated softwoods that are naturally rot resistant, including redwood and cedar, are still available, but prices are rising as supply declines. Heartwood of both is very stable for outdoor use and resists both decay and insects. Redwood is most widely available on the West Coast but can be special-ordered elsewhere. Both western red and Alaskan cedar are good choices for any location, although they are native to the West as well.

Tropical hardwoods such as ipé, cambara, and meranti are becoming popular for deck planking. All are attractive, durable, and rot resistant, but you may have to special-order them. Watch for imported woods that are certified by the Forest Stewardship Council, an international organization that has developed standards for responsible forest management.

Railings don't have to be wood. A steel railing makes for improved child safety on this deck cantilevered over a hillside. The steel also allows for the bold curve that mimics the bow of a ship.

At the deck corner, mitered pieces of 2-by-6 redwood create an inverted pyramid table that also conceals low-voltage lighting mounted underneath.

A favored low-maintenance alternative to wood, composite decking is also valued for its flexibility. Here it is used to curve around a tree.

More complex patterns—herringbone or parquetlike squares, for instance—are possible, though all require careful planning and require more decking due to waste. But regardless of the pattern, always follow two rules: framing should support the ends of every piece of decking, and no piece of decking should exceed its allowable span.

Plastic decking is available as all plastic or composite decking— recycled plastic mixed with sawdust or other natural material that lends a more woodlike look to the plank. Composite decking is solid; some plastic decking is hollow-core and uses proprietary fastening systems. None of these materials splinters, cracks, or rots.

Fasteners represent only a small portion of the cost of a deck, but it pays to invest in the best. Screws are far superior to nails, and stainless-steel, though more expensive than galvanized, lasts a lifetime and won't leave rust stains on the wood. Use two fasteners at each joist no matter the width of the decking.

decking

A deck's boards can be installed in a wide variety of patterns. All but the simplest require adjustments in the spacing of the framing, so you'll have to decide early in the process how you want the surface to look.

The simplest style has the decking boards running parallel to each other and to the house. It's easy to design and install and doesn't divert attention from the house, railings, or view. Introduce a subtle pattern by alternating plank widths, laying first a 2 by 6, then a 2 by 4, and so on.

If you'd prefer to have planks running perpendicular or at an angle to the house, it's necessary to rotate the understructure so that planks are still supported by the joists.

railings

Any deck more than 30 inches above the ground requires a railing, which needs to be 36 to 42 inches high, depending upon local codes, with sturdy balusters $3\frac{1}{2}$ to 4 inches apart that are bolted to framing. Beyond safety, railings can contribute an important design element.

When planning, consider the view from indoors. If your property allows, set the main surface of the deck a few steps below the house's floor level. Three steps, at 7 inches apiece, will keep the railing out of sightlines. If this isn't possible, consider railing panels of tempered glass or so-called airplane cable—plastic-coated wire cable—that is stretched between posts.

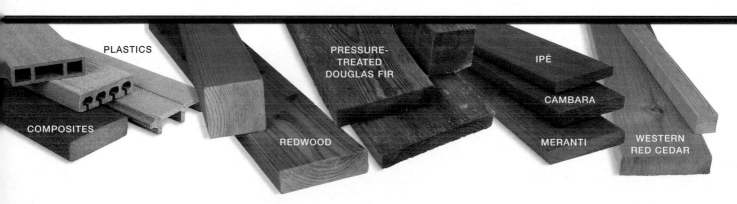

PLASTICS

COMPOSITES

PRESSURE-TREATED DOUGLAS FIR

REDWOOD

IPÉ

CAMBARA

MERANTI

WESTERN RED CEDAR

patios

A simple rectangular patio off the back door may be your best design option if you have a small, flat lot. But most often you can expand a patio in almost any direction and shape. If you create it from natural materials that blend with the house, it will project a sense of permanence and tradition.

You might also consider a detached, protected patio in a corner of your lot or a series of interrelated patios connected by steps. A neglected side yard may be the spot for a private, screened sitting area. Or an existing driveway could be converted with concrete "turf blocks" interplanted with lawn to soften the drive's appearance yet allow for traffic. Planted areas between flagstones or pavers can achieve a similar effect. Enclosed by a gate and landscaped, the driveway could double as an entry courtyard.

Patios needn't be large. This intimate and private spot is just big enough for a picnic table. Surrounded by plants, it blends seamlessly into the garden.

design

Track the sun's path and effect on the site as you plan your patio, remembering that masonry will absorb and reflect much more heat through the course of a summer day than a deck or lawn. If the site is exposed, consider interplanting or combining decking. But if the site is shaded, masonry can be cooling.

Also remember that whether you lay it, set it, or pour it in place, a patio requires edging. Repeat the chosen edging material elsewhere to visually link elements in the landscape. Edgings can also connect different areas in a garden. A brick-edged patio, for example, may taper off to a brick path.

Edgings include traditional brick, elegant stone, metal, and even plastic. Concrete pavers are rising stars, and they're easy for the do-it-yourselfer to install.

Like a deck, your patio should be an extension of your house's design, in both proportions and materials used. For ideas to mimic, study your house for patterns or details, such as trim, and look to window and door dimensions for a guide to scale.

When space is not a limiting factor, consider locating a patio as a quiet retreat away from the house, in a naturally cool and shaded area. Here, only the cushions move indoors for winter; the teak furniture stays out.

Houses like this L-shaped one cry out for a patio to link the ends. The mortared brick patio leaves plenty of space for planting beds, including a center one around an oak for shade.

Walled patios are natural extensions of indoor space and afford a similar sense of privacy. This one, with its whimsical, ornamented door, also reflects the artistry and tastes of the owners.

Low walls—complete with a decorative window—create a feeling of enclosure without shutting out the desert beyond. Decomposed granite fills large gaps left between irregularly shaped flagstone pavers. River rock simulates a creekbed and doubles as a drainage channel.

A functional patio for a family of four needs about 400 square feet. But some designers suggest making the patio the same size as the dominant adjacent indoor room. In that way, a connection between the house and patio is automatically made. Other techniques to relate the patio to the house include lining up the patio edges with a window, door, or corner of the house.

Keep the patio design simple and avoid awkward corners. One easy way to do that is to limit yourself to no more than two materials; this lends a sense of design harmony and connects the house to the patio.

A patio elevated on a bed of sand and gravel makes an elegant earth-bound transition between the house and the lawn.

Unlike decks, which are level, a patio must be graded so that water moves away from the house. This grade should be at least ⅛ inch per foot. So a patio that extends 24 feet from the house should be at least 3 inches lower at the far end.

materials

Paving options for patios include various masonry pavers, poured concrete, and loose materials such as gravel and wood chips. The choice depends mainly on whether you prefer a formal or an informal look. Brick, cut and sized stone, and cobblestones look formal if laid in a symmetrical pattern. Irregular flagstones or mossy bricks laid in sand achieve a softer, cottage-garden look, as do spaced concrete pavers filled with creeping plants.

Smooth poured concrete—the first choice for many patios of the past—is still widely used, probably because it's affordable, versatile, and durable. Concrete takes on a more modern and interesting look when textured, stamped with a pattern to look like stones or pavers, colored, or topped with exposed aggregate. You can also leave plant pockets in forming a slab and use curves liberally.

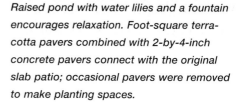

A mossy stone patio intersects a mulch path leading from the house to the garden. Informality and the natural materials chosen for paving and furnishings harmonize with the woodland surroundings.

A slab of concrete needs a firm base: at least 4 to 6 inches of compacted gravel. To keep from cracking, the slab itself needs to be 4 inches thick and reinforced with steel mesh.

Because paving materials—brick, stone, and individual concrete pavers—are heavy and expensive to move, the selection you'll be choosing from will

Raised pond with water lilies and a fountain encourages relaxation. Foot-square terra-cotta pavers combined with 2-by-4-inch concrete pavers connect with the original slab patio; occasional pavers were removed to make planting spaces.

probably all be from your region of the country. Fortunately, natural materials such as stone quarried locally look more appropriate than those from a different region.

After stone, brick and concrete pavers are next in popularity. Some of these materials can be combined to create patterns. Since brick is less expensive than stone, you might consider it for a walk that leads to a stone patio bordered with the same brick.

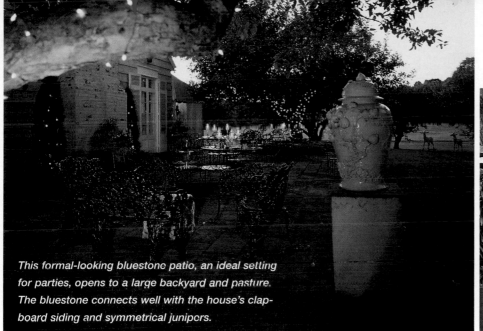

This formal-looking bluestone patio, an ideal setting for parties, opens to a large backyard and pasture. The bluestone connects well with the house's clapboard siding and symmetrical junipers.

In cool areas, providing shade may be less important than retaining heat. This masonry patio soaks up the sun's heat all day, then radiates it in the evening. When even that fails, a backup heater comes to the rescue.

Paving stones are rocks that are quarried in flat, thin sheets. Slate and sandstone, often grouped as flagstone, are common examples. Irregularly shaped stone lends a more casual look, while stone cut in rectangular sections is more formal. Color variation is natural in stone. When you're shopping for it, set out several pieces together to get a more realistic sense of what a large expanse will look like. Also, individual pieces will have different shapes and thicknesses. As a result, it takes longer to lay and level stone than to lay consistently sized pavers.

Bed preparation is key. The most permanent bed is a 4-inch-thick concrete slab poured onto a gravel base. The stone is then set on top in a bed of mortar. However, if a permanent border is established so the stone can't spread, it can be laid in sand.

Concrete pavers provide a hard, even surface, and many colors and shapes are available to complement your house. Like brick, concrete pavers rely on a permanent border and a well-compacted bed. Create the permanent border first, then a base of 4 inches of compacted gravel topped with at least 1 inch of compacted bedding sand. Replacing stained or broken pavers installed this way is easier than when mortared in place.

Brick looks natural in a garden and is also relatively affordable. Salvaged brick costs a bit more than new, but has an antique warmth. New and salvaged bricks classed as "MW" should be used in mild-winter climates only. In the North, use hard, "severe weathering" bricks (classified as "SX") for paving.

PAVING STONES

CONCRETE PAVERS

BRICK

Fitting together large, irregular bluestones is an art. Joined stones make a broad swath through a large garden, toward a stone bench, and around a boulder.

paths

All gardens have paths, planned or otherwise. A well-designed path keeps your feet dry and makes coming and going easy and safe. Paths also link the house to the garden, visually as well as physically. But a great path does much more. Whether it directs you and your guests under an archway of jasmine or around a bend to a reflecting pool, paths make the garden more inviting. A successful path also shapes and defines garden areas as it connects unrelated parts of the landscape to create a coherent whole.

The most interesting paths provide different experiences along the way. For instance, at a curve—where a guest might naturally pause—an interesting shrub or perhaps a view claims a glance. Paths can reveal special plantings, a piece of sculpture, a small bench, or a pleasing scene. A path that curves and disappears around a corner arouses curiosity about what lies beyond.

A path is best when it curves around something. If the path changes direction, place a plant, stone, or bench at the point where it turns, so the turn will have a reason for being.

How wide should a path be? It depends on how it will be used. If it winds discreetly through the garden and serves only as a walking surface, 2 feet is the minimum. To allow room for lawn mowers and wheelbarrows, make it at least 3 feet wide. For two people to walk abreast, as on an entry path, it should be 5 feet wide. To make entry walks particularly inviting, make them even wider.

Flagstone steppingstones follow the lawn's curve and lead to a shaded bench. The stones, though irregular, are similarly shaped; 4- to 6-inch-wide gaps left between stones allow gray woolly thyme to fill in.

A ring of poured concrete serves as a walkway around a patch of lawn. The herringbone brick path connects the ring to the driveway, then continues under the distant gate.

creating illusions

When you design a path, try to create illusions that can enhance your garden.

■ If space is limited and you want the garden to seem larger, obscure the pathway's end. Or use "forced perspective" by subtly diminishing the width of the path to make it appear bigger.

■ Straight, narrow paths can make a garden appear longer, especially if the end point is hidden.

■ A curving path, or one laid on the diagonal, draws the eye from side to side and makes the journey look more interesting.

ABOVE RIGHT: Square exposed-aggregate concrete pavers point the way from gate to patio. Note how the pavers' orientation shifts. RIGHT: A steppingstone path leading from the lawn to a serene setting provides a strong connection between separate parts of the landscape.

■ In yards dominated by lawn, steppingstone paths break up and add interest to the expanse of green, protecting the grass from wear and tear. Set them low enough to mow over.

materials

When choosing materials for your path, consider safety, practicality, appearance, and cost. The choices, ranging between rough cobbles and wood rounds, are many. Another choice is lumber—redwood or cedar decking atop a pressure-treated base, or pressure-treated timbers laid side by side.

A path that fits in visually is made of materials that blend with the style

Switching from flagstone to brick adds visual variety and saves money. Repeating the flagstones just before the corner continues the transition between the two materials and makes it feel less abrupt.

of the house and surrounding structures. That doesn't mean you can't mix in contrasting materials to perk it up. Mixing also helps save money by blending less expensive materials with more costly ones.

Unless you've chosen a highly porous, quick-draining material such as gravel, plan to pitch the path slightly to one side, or build it with a slight crown in the center. For rain to run off, the path needs a grade of about ⅛ inch of slope per foot.

Gravel and crushed stone make low-cost, fast-draining surfaces. Both are available in a range of colors and sizes, and they are relatively easy to install. Gravel is sold in bags and in bulk by the ton or cubic yard. Bulk stone costs less than bagged, although

This naturalistic path emulates a woodland trail where the idea is to meander slowly. Because wood chip and bark mulch paths are impermanent, they are inexpensive and simple to create.

Traditional brick patterns are fine, but you can invent your own, too. This one uses three vertical and three horizontal courses that guide the walker, but not overtly.

Brick can be laid in countless patterns and is relatively affordable. It requires little maintenance and is easy to work with. Choose a basic end-on-end pattern like running bond or stack bond for curved paths to avoid extensive brick cutting (see illustration below). And always use paving bricks, not wall bricks; they're harder and more durable. For safety's sake, choose bricks with a rough surface. Install a stout steel or plastic edging to contain them and prevent them from spreading. Costs range from 45 to 65 cents each, or $2 to $3 per square foot.

Cut or irregular stone makes an elegant path surface, but it's also the most expensive and among the most challenging to lay. It's sold by masonry suppliers and is available in irregular shapes or cut to uniform size, typically squares or rectangles sized in 6-inch increments. Native stone blends well with the surroundings. Expect to pay at least $3 to $4 per square foot.

delivery is extra. Prices vary, but expect to pay anywhere between $8 and $80 or more a ton, enough to cover 100 square feet 2 inches deep.

Bridge or walkway? Either way, the path makes a compelling entrance that keeps to the house's Japanese style. Heavy planks and railings permit confident steps and encourage guests to linger and take in the view.

BRICK PATTERNS

(Clockwise from top left) BASKET WEAVE: Requires bricks that are exactly half as wide as long. A deep vertical soldier course stabilizes edges. RUNNING BOND: Alternate rows are aligned. HERRINGBONE: Requires the most brick cutting, because edges need a half brick every foot. COLONIAL WILLIAMSBURG: Accommodates bricks of varying sizes, as the rows are not linked to each other.

fences and gates

No other garden element performs as many duties as a fence does. Fences transform a garden into a secure, attractive retreat from the outside world. They keep strangers out, and children and pets in; they also go up fast, providing instant privacy. And if you choose materials well and build carefully, a fence is relatively easy to maintain and will last for decades to come.

Wherever space is limited, a fence is a practical choice compared to hedges and masonry walls that do many of the same jobs but need more width. A 6- to 8-foot-high fence needs only about a foot of horizontal space along its length. A block wall of the same height needs at least twice as much, and a hedge considerably more.

A scalloped white picket fence is an American classic, with slant-cut pickets and ball post caps. Low fences like this one establish a boundary but still welcome visitors with their openness.

You might not need to surround your entire yard to gain privacy. Fence sections cut the expense and work but still create privacy and separate outdoor spaces. Interior fences can divide your yard into areas for recreation, relaxation, gardening, and storage. Because

This privacy fence jogs to accommodate sloping ground: top and bottom rails remain level. The lattice top, while extending the fence slightly, makes it less imposing and creates space for climbing plants.

partitions create more places to explore, they make a garden feel somewhat larger.

Where the ground slopes, decide whether you want the fence to follow the slope or jog up or down to conform to the ground contour while keeping rails level. It's often a matter of style: rustic fences are expected to follow the land, while a more formal fence is expected either to be level or to jog uniformly. In general, the balance of a garden is skewed somewhat when the main reference point in the background—the fence—is uneven.

Select fence styles carefully. A solid-board fence blocks the view completely, but it cuts out light. It also cuts the wind close by, but wind just a few feet away can swirl down over the top of the fence and feel even stronger. A fence with airspaces that slow the wind, but

Following the garden's casual, natural style, this rail fence was made of branches pruned from nearby trees.

don't stop it, is better at taming wind than a solid one.

If you'd prefer your fence to be unobtrusive, make it plain and mask it with plants. Place shrubs in front of it, or train a vine along the top. You can also paint it a deep green or gray-green so that it blends into the shrubbery in front of it.

Most communities have regulations restricting fence height. In many places, the maximum allowable height is 3½ feet for front-yard fences and 6 feet for backyard fences. Tall fences are also more difficult to build and require more material. An alternative way to gain height is to train a plant to clothe the top of a fence, or plant narrow trees or shrubs in front of it.

As a courtesy to your neighbors, choose a fence design that looks good on their side as well as on your own. In fact, some communities require "good neighbor" fencing, with boards mounted on alternating sides. In such cases, the boundary fence may be owned and maintained by both neighbors. Whatever the rules, make every effort to come to a friendly agreement with your neighbors on the location, design, and construction of the fence.

FENCE STYLES

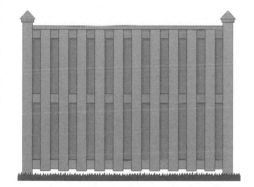

ALTERNATING SLAT FENCE, 6 FEET HIGH
High enough for screening and considerable privacy; small openings between slats allow air flow but eliminate view into yard.

TULIP-TOP PICKET FENCE, 4 FEET HIGH
Defines a property border without blocking the view. Can keep a small dog in the yard; also useful to define areas within a yard or to serve as backdrop for plants.

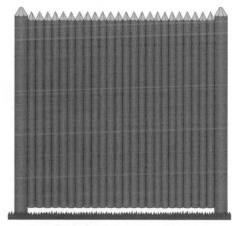

RUSTIC STOCKADE FENCE, 8 FEET HIGH
Lack of footholds and sharp pickets provide some security, and close spacing blocks views, increasing privacy.

BELOW: Through one window to another: carefully crafted custom gates are open enough to allow passersby a partial view inside but are substantial enough to block browsing animals.

If you're replacing an existing fence, boundary questions are unlikely. But if you're putting up a first-time fence and aren't sure of the boundary, hire a licensed surveyor to find it, referring to town records as needed. Then build the fence an inch or two inside your property line so that you have total control over it. But don't leave too much of your plot on the other side, because, over time, fences become the "boundary by estoppel"—a legal term that means the fence can lead other people to believe that the fence itself is the boundary.

materials

Most fences are built of the same basic components: vertical 4-by-4 posts set into the ground, 2-by-4 horizontal rails that connect the posts and support the vertical components, and facing boards or lattice panels, usually of 1-by lumber. Depending

ABOVE: A partial fence screens out pool equipment and supplies. Oversized and detailed capped posts and custom 1-by-2 lattice panels make the structure substantial yet nonintrusive.

upon the fence height and the design, posts are set at least 3 feet into the ground and no more than 8 feet apart. Some builders anchor each post with concrete from a couple of sacks of concrete mix, but Roger Cook disagrees, explaining that the concrete serves only to trap moisture and speed decay. He sets the post on an inch or two of gravel and then packs earth hard around the post.

Most fences are built partly or entirely of wood, but only the toughest woods can survive the elements. Pressure-treated posts—rated for ground contact with a preservative retention level of 0.40 pounds of preservative per cubic foot—and rails last longest for the price,

although the look of redwood and cedar are preferred. For face boards, redwood or cedar can be left natural, while other materials like spruce and pine have to be stained or painted to last. Use weather-resistant fasteners: hot-dipped galvanized steel nails or screws at a minimum, stainless steel if you can afford it.

Wood's versatility as a fencing material is reflected in its wide variety of forms—split rails, grape stakes, dimension lumber, pickets, and poles. Alternative materials include plastic, galvanized wire, plastic mesh, and ornamental iron. Vinyl fences, although initially quite expensive, are readily available and are easy to maintain and install.

Painted fences are charming but require scraping and repainting every five years or so. Opaque stains don't last as long as paint, but they demand less prep work when it's time for a new coat. Transparent stains are the easiest to apply and maintain because they soak into the wood instead of creating a brittle film on the surface. The simplest treatment: leave the wood to weather to gray and blend with the landscape.

Whatever your choice of fencing, coordinate the fence with the style and materials of your house. A picket fence would be too dainty for a contemporary stone-and-glass house, but it could look fine with

An opening in a hedge gives a whimsical look to this gate. The effect is enhanced by training the hedge to go over the top in the shape of the gate.

a colonial brick or clapboard structure. Louvered or solid board fences, however, can complement a variety of house styles.

choosing a gate

Place a gate where you need access, to frame a view, or even to make a design statement in tandem with the fence. You may want to build the gate in a style and with material that matches the fence, but you can also choose a contrasting material or design, such as a wooden or wrought-iron gate flanked by brick posts.

The minimum width for a gate is usually 3 feet, but an extra foot creates a more gracious feeling. If you anticipate moving equipment through the gate, you'll appreciate all the extra inches added to the opening. For an extra-wide space, consider a two-part gate or even a gate on rollers designed for a driveway. Use 6-by-6 posts set deeper into the soil for extra rigidity, and weather-resistant, heavy hinge hardware with long screws. Concrete is often recommended for gate posts by builders who don't use it elsewhere.

Most gates sag over time, rubbing against their hinge post or dragging on the ground. This is because they have come out of square. The best gates use mortise-and-tenon diagonal braces to prevent this, but you can fix the problem by using cable and tensioners.

These weighty, durable masonry pillars are more than adequate support for the gate. Artful flower cutouts provide a glimpse of the garden beyond.

walls

Like fences and hedges, walls establish boundaries and create privacy. But they can do more. Walls can assume shapes, curves, or architectural themes that are impossible with fences and hedges. Low walls can provide seating, while taller ones can block noise. A wall's heft and strength make the garden feel more permanent and timeless. But perhaps most significantly, walls are strong enough to hold back soil.

Once you've determined why you need a wall, you should choose its location, height, and width, and the degree of visual screening it will provide. You'll also need to select materials that coordinate with the style and design of your house and any existing garden structures.

Typical wall materials include bricks or concrete block, uncut stone, and poured concrete. With bricks or block, you can choose a decorative pattern for laying the courses, incorporate a solid or an openwork face, vary the thickness, cover the materials with stucco to produce a smooth surface, and even incorporate glass-block sections to let light pass through.

In the hands of an experienced mason, stone can be used to create walls that appear to have grown out of the soil.

Poured concrete offers more design possibilities because surface texture and shape are established by wood forms. Most of the work goes into constructing and stabilizing these forms; the actual concrete pour is accomplished quickly.

Before beginning any wall, ask your building department about regulations that specify how high and how close to your property line you can build, what kind of foundation you'll need, and whether the wall requires steel reinforcement. Many municipalities require a building permit for any masonry wall more than 3 feet high. Some require that the wall be approved by an engineer.

seating walls

Around a patio, a seat wall makes the space more intimate by enclosing it without blocking views. A height of 18 to 22 inches is comfortable to sit on, though the finished height is usually a function of the material used to

Shutters around a wall opening fool the eye, letting you see "out" from both directions. A young southern magnolia and a blooming azalea accent the painted brick.

A mortared free-standing brick wall, rising naturally from a brick patio, adds to the patio's privacy. Gaps between the cap bricks form tiny pockets for plants.

build the wall. Seating walls can include lighting or electrical outlets, and—if the grade beyond is higher—can double as retaining walls.

When the top or coping-stone layer is for seating it makes sense for those stones to overhang the wall by 1 to 1½ inches on all sides, so that water dripping off won't run down the face of the wall. Coping stones are often pitched slightly so that water will run off in a predictable direction.

retaining walls

You can tame a gentle slope with a single low retaining wall or a series of garden steps that hold the surface soil in place. But if your slope is long and steep, consider building two or three substantial walls to divide it into terraces, which you can then enhance with plantings.

Stones fit together tightly and artfully create a retaining wall with built-in bench. Flagstones form the bench seat, and a heart-shaped fragment in the seat back provides a personal touch.

Terraced retaining walls of poured concrete form planting beds, filled here with yellow-flowered kangaroo paws (Anigozanthos), lavender-flowered society garlic, New Zealand flax, and grasses.

Engineering aside, you can build a retaining wall from any of the materials suggested for standard walls: bricks or blocks, uncut stone, and poured concrete. Wood is another option, in the form of treated wood timbers.

On a low, stable slope, you can lay uncut stones or chunks of broken concrete without mortar or footings. Fill the soil-lined crevices with colorful plantings.

New systems for building concrete-block retaining walls don't require you to mix a single bag of mortar. These walls are built with precast modules that stack or lock together with clips, pins, or friction. They are ideal for building 3- to 4-foot-high walls (see pages 112–115).

In all cases, make sure there is adequate drainage behind a retaining wall to handle hydrostatic pressure.

Otherwise, as water accumulates behind the wall, it will create enough pressure to cause the wall to fail. It is critical that you allow water a means to escape. In some cases, weep holes are sufficient, but you are much safer laying perforated drain tile just behind the wall.

Many cities require foundations under mortared walls, so check the code requirements in your area. Because mortar absorbs moisture, it should not have continuous contact with soil, especially in colder climates. When wet mortar freezes, the mortar cracks.

Normally the foundation must be below the frost line, which is a matter of inches in the South but may be 4 feet or more in cold-winter climates.

landscape lighting

Tiny spots of light draw the eye, stretch the view, and subtly make a small garden feel larger. Broad swaths of light from low fixtures on both sides of the steps make them easier to navigate.

Evening is often the best time to enjoy your landscape. Temperatures are down, the responsibilities of the day are past, and it's more likely that friends and family can join you. Enjoyed under lights, the garden takes on a whole new dimension.

As you start thinking about lighting, decide how it will be used. Think about which features to highlight and which are better left in the dark. Lighting professionals distinguish two different types of lighting: functional lighting, for safety or specific tasks or activities; and accent lighting, for dramatic effect.

functional lighting

It's widely known and accepted that lighting can increase safety. Small lights that show steps or other changes in the footpath are essential in many situations. Floodlights, sometimes connected to a movement-sensing switch, discourage intruders.

Task lights brighten areas, especially where cooking is done, and they make sense in places where you or your family pursues regular activities. Consider

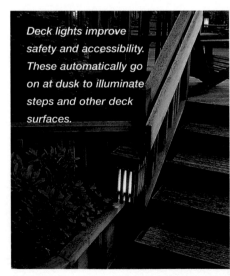

Deck lights improve safety and accessibility. These automatically go on at dusk to illuminate steps and other deck surfaces.

floodlights for badminton on the lawn, shooting hoops, swimming, or for tending the vegetable garden at night.

Functional lighting will provide the most benefit if the fixtures are close to the ground and produce broad pools of light.

accent lighting

Don't discount the benefits of lighting for dramatic effect. Accent lighting may lack any straightforward utility that makes its cost easy to justify, but it's more than just decoration.

Landscape lighting isn't just about being outdoors; it's also about how you see the garden from indoors at night. If you peer out at an unlit garden, the windows you're peering out of will seem like dark mirrors. Landscape lighting makes the windows transparent again.

Conversely, too much lighting will look forced and be more of an intrusion than a delight. Be aware that too much light carelessly thrown about

Light reflected off the wall silhouettes a starkly lit eucalyptus. Grazing lights at the tree's sides reveal the rough and peeling bark, and accent the lower branches.

is a pollutant and is likely to annoy neighbors. Try for the subtle effects that small amounts of light can produce. Leaving some areas in shadow actually enhances their mystery.

As you might expect, the subtlety required of accent lights has encouraged the development of subcategories, shown at right. When you understand what they do, you'll be able to develop your own lighting plan. In all cases, look for simple, unfussy fixtures that disappear into the garden.

planning systems

Most landscape lighting systems operate on 12 volts and are called "low voltage." And the heart of low-voltage lighting systems is the transformer. Choose one based on the total number of watts needed for the system (the sum of all the lamps used) plus 25 percent, so the transformer doesn't operate at full capacity. To allow for future expansion, buy a transformer with 50 percent greater capacity. A typical 300-watt transformer, large enough for 12 lamps at 20 watts each, costs about $300. But variations are many: some can power multiple circuits, some include timers, and some are made for direct burial.

Direct-burial lighting cable is either 12, 10, or 8 gauge, with the smaller gauges indicating larger size. Costs range from 30 cents for 12 gauge, to 90 cents per foot for 8 gauge.

SHADOW LIGHTS are bright and aimed at the subject. They cast a broad enough beam to throw a magnified shadow onto a nearby wall.

UPLIGHT FIXTURES are mounted low and aimed upward, usually into the branches of a tree. The undersides of branches are illuminated, and the topmost canopy reflects the light's glow.

MOONLIGHTS provide dim light and are mounted high in trees, imitating the light of the moon and creating soft pools of light on the ground.

SPOTLIGHTS are what you'd expect: lights focused on a special plant, pot, sculpture, or focal point. The light source may be either below or above the object.

BACKLIGHTS are situated behind an object, such as a tree, and the light is directed toward viewers. The result is a dramatic silhouette.

GRAZING LIGHTS are aimed nearly parallel to the surface, to accent its irregularity or texture. The surface is usually a wall or fence, but it may also be a tree or the surface of a pond.

arbors and gazebos

Extending from the house and over the patio, this arbor, with widely spaced rafters, is designed to support vines, which by summer create a shady retreat.

A partially enclosed garden structure is a refuge from household bustle—a place to sit quietly or to host a party on a warm evening. It provides shade during the day and shelter during cool evenings, yet it is open to breezes and garden views.

Arbors and gazebos play decorative and practical roles in the garden. They can support climbing plants, tie together garden areas, define zones of use, direct foot traffic, and mask a plain or unsightly feature.

To find the best site for the structure, walk around your property, glancing back at the house. Look for a vantage point that provides long, diagonal views across the garden. Consider which exposure you want. For example, if your main deck or patio is in full sun, you may prefer a shady corner.

Then start to think about the design of the structure as well as the walkway leading to it, which can add to the view. Make the route to your hideaway direct or circuitous; mark the spot itself with a clearly visible overhead structure, or use subtle screening and tall plantings as camouflage.

Arbors are literally defined as latticework covered by shrubs or vines. They tend to be sizable structures that afford peaceful shelter in which to relax and reflect. Generally rendered less imposing by simple design and graceful arches, arbors can be partly attached to a house wall or roof or can be freestanding, colonnade-style.

This rustic freestanding arbor marks the transition from lawn to patio space. Its tree-limb timbers, covered by morning glories, reinforce the untamed style of the garden.

A departure from the traditional style, this gazebo's ceiling of molded acrylic panels makes for dry summer seating and provides sunlight for plants. Removable glass sides make it a conservatory during winter.

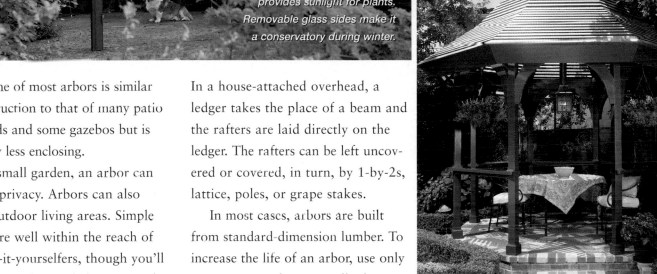

An updated traditional-design gazebo features a louvered roof and, to enhance the view of the rose garden, a raised brick floor. The pendant light fixture and built-in stereo speakers encourage casual night-time gatherings.

The frame of most arbors is similar in construction to that of many patio overheads and some gazebos but is generally less enclosing.

In a small garden, an arbor can provide privacy. Arbors can also define outdoor living areas. Simple arbors are well within the reach of most do-it-yourselfers, though you'll probably need some help to raise the heaviest structural beams into place.

The key to arbor design is its criss-cross or stacking quality: each new layer is placed perpendicular to the one below it. Although you build an overhead from the ground up, you should design it from the top down. First choose the kind of overhead structure you want. That decision will influence the size and spacing of the support members below.

Whether free-standing or attached to a building, an arbor is held up by a series of posts or columns. These support horizontal beams, which in turn support rafters.

In a house-attached overhead, a ledger takes the place of a beam and the rafters are laid directly on the ledger. The rafters can be left uncovered or covered, in turn, by 1-by-2s, lattice, poles, or grape stakes.

In most cases, arbors are built from standard-dimension lumber. To increase the life of an arbor, use only pressure-treated or naturally decay-resistant materials, such as redwood or cedar heartwood. Open arbors don't collect much rain or snow, so they need to support only the weight of the materials themselves, plus the weight of any plants growing on them. For added lateral strength, brace the structure where the posts meet the beams.

Gazebos are free-standing roofed structures that are usually open on the sides. They can be romantic retreats or destinations, or serve the more prosaic function of screening undesirable views.

Traditional gazebos have either six or eight sides and sloping rafters joined in a central hub at the roof peak. Often the hexagonal or octagonal sides are partly enclosed with lath, lattice, or even metal grillwork. Newer, looser interpretations can be husky, with hefty corner columns and stacked beams, or quite airy, consisting of little more than four posts connected by pairs of 2-by-6s. Several designs are available as prefab kits, greatly simplifying construction.

pools and spas

A backyard swimming pool used to be a pretty predictable affair, but homeowners can now choose from a variety of new surfacing materials, high-tech lights and filters, and features such as reefs and fountains and many other extras—all intended to make the backyard pool more like a vacation destination.

Pools and spas are often the perfect backyard entertainment. But be forewarned: they are expensive and require maintenance. Their novelty may also wear off fast, sometimes after only a few years.

Make your pool suit your needs and your tastes. Children need a wide, shallow area; lap swimmers require a long, straight section. Unless it will be used for diving, a pool need not be deeper than 4 to 5 feet. For lap swimming, one long axis, preferably 30 feet, will suffice; the width can be as little as 7 or 8 feet.

Try to locate the pool in a private spot in full sun. There should be clear access from the pool to a changing room and bathroom. You'll also want it to be convenient to reach—and easy to light—in the evening.

To emphasize the retro curves of this updated 1950s pool, the owners chose a narrow stone surround rather than more practical, broader decking.

Water cascading over boulders takes advantage of the slope leading down to a small tiled pool that includes an attached spa.

Allow for paving or decking around the pool, ideally with a non-skid surface. Add boulders, flagstones, bridges, and other free-form edgings and your pool can double as a garden pond.

Pool equipment includes a pump, heater, and filter. You'll need to provide a concrete slab to support them, ideally screened from both sight

One variation on the lap pool is the flume pool. Against its adjustable current, swimmers stroke forward but stay in place, reaping the benefit of a much larger pool.

and sound. If you have the space, place the slab between 25 and 50 feet from the pool: any closer and you'll hear the noise; any farther and you'll need larger equipment to pump water the extra distance.

pool construction

Pools can be built aboveground or completely or partly in-ground. Fully in-ground pools are typically accessed from patios.

For the structure, concrete (usually sprayed as Gunite or Shotcrete and reinforced with steel) combines workability, strength, permanence, and flexibility of design. Interior finishes include paint, plaster, and tile, in ascending order of cost. To keep the price down, save tile for details—edgings, step markers, and around the waterline. Use glass tiles or pebble aggregate to add glimmer and texture.

Vinyl-lined pools are usually much less expensive than concrete styles because materials cost less and installation is quicker. The liner generally rests on a bed of sand and is supported by walls made of aluminum, steel, plaster, concrete block, or wood. These walls can extend above grade, making them especially economical for sloping sites. Vinyl is not as durable as concrete, but leaks can be repaired.

Fiberglass pools consist of a one-piece rigid fiberglass shell supported by a bed of sand. These pools are fairly quick to install, but the choices of pool shapes and sizes are limited.

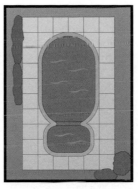

SPLASH POOL features a shallow, sloping "beach entry" for small children.

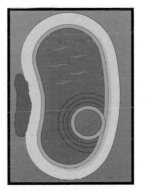

FREE-FORM POOL is an all-purpose type, but you can determine its shape.

SPORTS POOL is 5 feet deep in the middle and 3 feet at the ends, good for games, aerobics, and lap swimming.

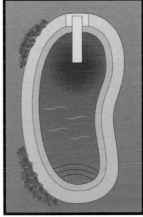

DIVING POOL includes a board and a deep end that's at least 7 feet deep.

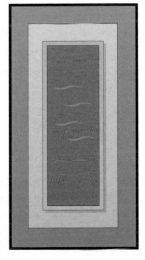

LAP POOL, which is 5 feet deep, 8 feet wide, and about 30 feet long, fits where other pools can't.

spas

Hot tubs and spas have the same function but differ in materials and form. Both use virtually identical support equipment to create hot, bubbling water.

Spas run the gamut of design choices, from boxy portable models to those of pool-sized proportions. A portable, self-contained spa doesn't have to be permanently installed and comes as a complete unit, ready to be plugged into a 120-volt outlet (or wired to a 240-volt circuit). Its support equipment is part of the package.

In-ground spas can be set into a hole dug into the ground or into an above-grade surface such as a deck that is supported by a concrete pad from below. Shopping for an in-ground spa means choosing between a factory-molded shell made of acrylic reinforced with fiberglass or high-impact thermoplastics, or a more expensive, longer-lasting shell made of concrete.

ponds and fountains

In Phoenix, a pond is an obvious addition to a garden. It's a powerful magnet for children, adults, birds, even dogs. But water is equally powerful in places where it isn't scarce, such as Seattle or Miami. While most of us take the power of water for granted in everyday life, in gardens we experience its soul-satisfying qualities directly.

There are other good reasons to include a pond, fountain, or both in your garden plans. One is the sound water makes. Whether it is from a formal pool or a babbling brook, the

Water lilies and koi add life to this naturalistic pond. Water recirculates gently through the urn and over its sides, enough movement for a very gentle sound. Plants nearly encircle the pond, obscuring the edge.

enticing sound of water brings a dynamic character to the garden. And don't forget the value of the plants and fish that live in water. They add a liveliness to the garden that's obtainable in no other way.

Large ponds alive with fish and plants are a joy, to be sure. But to enjoy water you don't need much. A bowl, perhaps with a recirculating bubbler, can make your garden more pleasurable than you might guess.

The obvious place for a pond is near the house, where it's easy to experience frequently. And because children find ponds irresistible, the safest locations are in fenced back-

yards. Usually, ponds less than 24 inches deep don't require a building permit, but check with your local building department about any requirements for property setbacks and fencing with self-latching gates.

Flexible pond liners are available at most garden centers to line excavated ponds. Use fish-safe, synthetic rubber liners—45-mil EPDM is the standard. Liners can be cut and, as

A metal grid supports the tightly fitted, vertically stacked flagstones, and a concrete footing supports the grid. Pond liner covers the excavated space below. The design was inspired by a chrysanthemum flower.

a last resort, solvent-welded to fit odd-shaped water features. But you can find EPDM in rolls large enough to fit most any pond size.

Another option is a preformed fiberglass shell. A number of shapes and sizes are available. If you intend to overwinter fish in a northern climate, look for a pond at least 24 inches deep. Although these cost more than synthetic rubber-lined pools, they usually last longer. For large ponds, use a Gunite shell, the most permanent (and expensive) of all.

The size of your pond will be restricted by the space available, but its shape and style are limited only by your imagination. If you wish to start small, consider the portable decorative pools available at garden centers and statuary stores, or create your own version.

If you're interested in moving water, you can choose between spray fountains, waterfalls, and spill fountains. Spray fountains are best suited to formal water features and are made versa-

A furnished patio provides the perfect vantage point to enjoy this 100,000-gallon pond, home to water lilies, iris, and three dozen koi.

Surrounded by hostas and camellias, this small Asian-inspired fountain surprises visitors. Though made of formed cement, tucked into this shady niche it looks as though nature set it there.

tile by assorted heads that shoot water in massive columns or lacy mists. Waterfalls send a cascade toward a pond from a simple outlet pipe. The water in spill or wall fountains flows from the outlet into a pool or series of tiered pans or shelves. These types of fountains are good choices for smaller gardens and can even stand alone.

If water plants or fish are on your list of desirables, consider several fac-

tors. Water plants will do well if in full sun and protected from strong winds. And if you can avoid placing a pond under or near a deciduous tree, by all means do so. Falling leaves will fill and clog a small pond. (But you can cover a pond under a deciduous tree with a length of lightweight plastic netting.)

Use native stones and boulders to border your pond in a natural fashion, ideally in combination with plants. Or use brick or flagstone laid in mortar on a wide concrete lip. You can also build decking around all or part of a pond.

kids' play spaces

Backyard garden space is a wonderful gift to children. How better to introduce them to nature than in the safety of your own enclosed yard?

To begin with the obvious, you'll need boundary fencing and fencing to keep kids from any potential danger. Kids' natural curiosity can't be contained, so fence off tools, garden supplies, and places you don't want them to go.

Part of planning play spaces for children is a function of their age. As common sense would dictate, keep very young children close to the house so they can be easily watched and heard. Sandboxes (covered when not in use) are a guaranteed hit, as is anything to do with water. But keep in mind that even shallow water can be a

One virtue of a play set is its efficiency. In a very small space kids can climb, jump, slide, and play scout from the platform.

danger for little ones. Don't include a pond or pool until the kids are older and reliable around water. Similarly, as you choose plants, avoid those that are thorny, and certainly any that are poisonous (see page 184).

Of all the opportunities you can provide for your children in the gar-

Creating a play space for the children was part of the initial design for this patio; so was being able to convert it to additional patio space in the post-sandbox days. Boulders and logs make excellent jumping platforms to occupy kids while parents relax close by.

den, perhaps the greatest is a space of their own. Screen it if you can, for at least the illusion of privacy, and so that their messes aren't an issue when company comes around. But for as long as supervision is critical, make the space easy to see from the house or an upper-story window.

Take sun, wind, and shade into account. Hot sun increases the risk of sunburn and can make metal slides or bars, as well as concrete walks, burning hot, so install slide surfaces facing north. If your property is in the path of strong winds, locate the play yard inside a windbreak of fencing or dense trees. Dappled shade is ideal. If you have no spreading foliage, position the play yard on the north side of your house, construct a simple canopy of lath or canvas, or plan a play structure that includes a shaded portion.

Many public playgrounds feature metal play structures rather than timber, because wood eventually rots. Still, wood is a warmer and friendlier material—and a good quality wooden structure will last as long as your children will use it at home. If you choose wood, make sure it is not treated with CCA preservative, which is being gradually phased out in favor of safer alternatives.

Allow at least 6 feet of space around all sides of swings, slides, and climbing structures for a fall zone, then cushion it well. Sand is probably the best, for its safety and entertainment value—unless you or your

neighbors own cats. In that case, take a cue from elementary school playgrounds, where interlocking rubber or foam mats are popular. Mulches of virgin wood last longer than bark and aren't hard on young feet. You'll need an edging to contain sand or mulch.

Lawn is perhaps the ideal play surface. But if it's going to take the abuse that older children can dish out, make sure to choose a grass that's tough enough and has some capacity to heal itself. In the south, that would be Bermuda grass; in the north, Kentucky blue. Keep in mind too that lawn and the desire to shade the play area are mutually exclusive. No lawn will survive for long under a swing or in a shaded area. Another caution is to avoid lawn seed mixtures that contain clover, creeping thyme, or the sometime weed called lippia. Bees love their flowers, and

there's no sense increasing the odds of a bee sting.

If your child is among the many fascinated by wheels and all toys that have them, a section of smooth concrete will get plenty of use. Consider making a circular path, at least 2 feet wide, so your child can ride round and round.

You can buy plans or kits for playhouses at home-improvement stores. (Some are designed to convert into potting sheds.) Nestle the playhouse into a secluded corner and landscape around it.

When children are little, it's difficult to imagine them growing up. But when they are older, you'll need an exit strategy for whatever play structure you've lived with for the past dozen years or so. Consider structures that can be converted to another use or removed with little difficulty.

If you have a handy wall, consider letting the kids turn it into an outdoor mural. This wall of concrete block is now the edge of an imaginary pond. The tree trunk is complete with a red gecko. Pots of trailing ice plant on the top of the wall bring the scene to life.

outdoor kitchens

Maybe it triggers some kind of ancestral memory of gathering around the fire, or maybe it's just the kid in us. But cooking—and eating—outside is just plain fun. Like magic, moving from inside to outside transforms just about any meal into a party.

Your climate has a large bearing not only on the specific design you choose but also on what it is reasonable to include. If outdoor living is a reality for you all year, or most of it, investing more in the outdoor dining option makes good sense.

RIGHT: Traditional themes define the design of this Tucson kitchen, where cooking and eating outdoors make sense more often than not. An African sumac tree (Rhus lancea) *casts dappled shade.*

In cool or windy areas, take advantage of existing protection, such as the side of the house, wall of the garage, potting shed, or corner where a wing meets the main house. The house itself provides some shelter for the appliances in winter, too. Fences or natural windscreens like hedges can reduce the influence of prevailing winds and provide late-afternoon shade.

LEFT: Locally quarried stone was used in this outdoor kitchen to pave the patio and face the concrete-block cooking islands. The ¾-inch countertops are edged to look as if they're a massive 3 inches thick.

For more practical reasons as well, the side of the house is an ideal location for an outdoor kitchen.

There's usually no need to excavate trenches for gas and electricity lines. (In cold climates, exterior water pipes must be either insulated or equipped with valves at low points to facilitate drainage in winter.) And when yard space is at a premium, an open space along the wall of the house might be the only spot available.

In addition to built-in cooking facilities, other amenities might include preparation and serving counters, storage cabinets, and perhaps a refrigerator and a sink. An advantage of these permanent installations over portable barbecues is that they usually run on piped-in natural gas rather than containers of propane or charcoal, which have to be resupplied occasionally.

Maintaining and cleaning outdoor cooking facilities can be a challenge. Materials make a difference. Glazed ceramic tiles, for example, are an excellent choice for countertops. Wood, on the other hand, should be avoided. Use protective grill covers and rugged materials such as concrete and tile so that you can clean the kitchen area simply by hosing it down. Place watertight electrical outlets out of the way of routine cleanup.

Install lighting much as you would for an indoor kitchen. Effective downlighting illuminates preparation areas; more diffuse fixtures, perhaps dimmer-controlled, can create the ambience desired for a dinner party. Decorative minilights or other accents add a background glow and provide safety when other lights are off.

Outdoor electrical outlets, light fixtures, and switches must be in watertight outdoor boxes; all outlets must also be protected by a ground fault circuit interrupter (GFCI), which shuts off power to the circuit in case of an electrical short.

A polished countertop of 1¼-inch-thick Canadian pine-green granite easily survives spills and cooking mishaps as well as anything weather dishes out.

This comprehensive L-shaped patio kitchen expands the home out to the backyard. The structure is made from concrete block surfaced with a veneer of half-thickness bricks manufactured to look used.

sheds, storage, and work areas

Start taking care of a yard and before you know it the tools and supplies are piling up. Usually such equipment winds up in the garage, which is fine as long as you can still get the car inside. If this scenario rings a bell, consider a garden shed. Sheds are surprisingly inexpensive and easy to build, and they are a good-looking and practical solution to the storage problem. An added counter surface can double as a potting shed and be even more functional.

Garden sheds and work spaces are, along with compost piles, usually tucked away behind a tree, a fence,

The smaller the garden, the more prominent the toolshed. A focal point itself, this centrally located "shed" shares design details and paint colors with the house.

or some kind of screening. But if you don't have that much available space, there are still ways to work a shed into your backyard.

Invest some effort in design and detail and you don't have to hide it. Next to a patio it will provide a better visual barrier than a fence, and give you easy access to everything inside. Some of the examples shown on these pages are quite a bit more than practical storage units. A compromise

A dream retreat for a gardener, this toolhouse and potting shed is tucked into a back corner, under shade trees. The extended gable overhang protects the potting table from rain, and tools are protected but are close to where they're needed.

This gardener's work center includes a potting table covered with galvanized sheet metal, shelves for tools and supplies, and plastic bins to hold potting soil.

easier to hang on nails. If you have potentially dangerous chemicals, include a lockable cabinet. A skylight is the easiest way to ensure good visibility inside, but electricity for a light (or the occasional power tool) is handy, too.

Look to your side yard to find space for a work table. Hinged lattice siding covers pull-out drawers and additional storage.

among all of these competing interests will result in the best possible location.

Before building a shed, be sure to check with your building department. If it is considered a permanent structure, you may need a permit, and its position may be limited by easements.

To figure out how big a shed you need, consider what you'll use the building for. For instance, if it will be mostly a potting shed, you'll probably want the door wide enough to move a wheelbarrow in and out easily. If the shed will be primarily for garden equipment and tools, measure the width and length of what you need to store before committing to a design. No matter how big you make your shed, it probably won't end up being big enough.

Building a shed is like building a house, but on a smaller scale. The basic approach is to design the shed to resemble the main house, taking into consideration its style and colors. Add decorative touches and visual interest to the front of a shed with shutters or shelves.

Extending the gables on one or both ends creates protected, useful space. Use it for a work table or perhaps a firewood rack.

Once the shell is built, focus on organizing the interior. If the structure will be used primarily as a garden shed, a countertop for potting and some cabinets for storage will be useful. Sheathing an interior wall with lengths of pegboard will provide numerous options for hanging tools and will make for a more finished look.

You can also install shelves and hooks for tools. Drill holes in handles of shovels and rakes to make them

Sheltered outdoor work centers that include a countertop for potting, bin storage, a sink, and racks or shelves for storage are much more preferable than ones inside, especially on those days when gardening is most attractive. Include tables customized for your specific needs; they may be free-standing or built against a wall or fence.

CHAPTER THREE

ground work

**FINALLY IT'S TIME TO PUT SHOVEL TO SOIL
AND BEGIN BUILDING YOUR LANDSCAPE**

ONCE YOUR LANDSCAPE PLAN IS COMPLETE, THE PHYSICAL work can begin. This entails clearing the area you're going to landscape of unwanted shrubs, trees, lawn, old fences, outbuildings—everything that doesn't fit in the new plan. By creating a clean plot to work on, you will be able to address drainage problems, plan for irrigation, and lay the groundwork for walkways and lighting, which is what this chapter covers.

A key part of site preparation is ensuring that water is always diverted away from your house and foundation by whatever means necessary, usually by grading but also by swales, berms, and underground drainage. Locate all services— underground and overhead—before digging, and be sure that any structures attached to the house, such as decks and trellises, meet building codes. From a broader perspective, be aware that there are federal, state, and local laws that protect wetlands, even vernal pools, which are seasonally flooded depressions that often contain rare plants. So check with local authorities before draining a low spot.

By doing a careful job at this stage of your landscaping project, you'll ensure that new structures and plants will last long after the dust settles.

site preparation

Just like the demolition that precedes an indoor remodeling project, redesigning a landscape requires that the site is cleared of unwanted lawns, trees, and shrubs. At the same time, you'll need to protect what you want to keep from the stresses of the construction process.

removing a lawn

To remove a small area of lawn, use a spade to cut below the roots and peel back the sod. Don't try to till sod into the soil; it results in clumps that are a nuisance to work around. If you plan to keep sod for transplanting, use a spade to cut strips.

For larger lawns, consider renting a gas-powered sod cutter, which slices 12- to 18-inch-wide swaths and features an adjustable depth-control mechanism for cutting below the roots.

If you'll be replanting sod, lay it out on plastic sheets, ideally in the shade, and water daily. To dispose of sod, check first to see if a neighbor needs any for patching. If not, add it to a compost pile or dispose of it in a debris box.

Removing a lawn is a three-step process. Roger Cook uses a sod cutter (left) to cut turf into manageable strips. He then cuts the strips into 6-foot lengths (top), and rolls them up into liftable pieces (bottom).

CALL BEFORE YOU DIG

Digging even a shallow ditch in your yard with a shovel presents some risks to buried utilities. But if you're going to use a backhoe to dig down several feet, be sure to confirm well in advance that there are no buried gas or electric lines. In most states, you must call gas and electric utilities 48 to 72 hours before you plan to dig. No central number covers all states, but if you have Internet access, virtually every state's one-call number is listed at http://www.underspace.com/refs/ocdir.shtml. Another useful source is **Underground Alert Services (USA)** at **(800) 642-2444**. In Maine, New Hampshire, Vermont, Massachusetts, and Rhode Island, dial **(888) 344-7233** to check on buried utilities.

removing trees

The first task is to cut down the unwanted tree. If you have it done professionally (strongly recommended if you don't have a lot of experience), ask the contractor for proof of liability insurance, licenses, and workers' compensation coverage. Also confirm in writing that the contractor will either haul away all the debris or cut the trunk and larger branches into firewood of a specific length.

Tree removal normally does not include stump removal. You can do this yourself, but not by digging it out. To remove a stump a foot or more in diameter requires a hole 4 feet across and nearly as deep.

The quick way to manage the job is with a stump grinder. This large machine literally chews a stump to pieces. It's not difficult to operate, but make sure the rental charge isn't nearly the same price as having the stump removed professionally.

If a stump will be under a deck or in another out-of-the-way place, you can simply cut it close to the ground and leave it. To speed stump decay somewhat, drill some holes into the stump and fill them with high-nitrogen fertilizer in order to promote the growth of decay microorganisms. But keep in mind that eventually the stump will rot and create a depression in the soil, if not a sinkhole.

For smaller stumps, expose the roots all around and cut them away with an ax, saw, or loppers. When

A wood chipper quickly chews up unwanted trees and shrubs to ready a site for relandscaping.

dealing with a taproot, dig deep enough to expose it and then chop through it. Once you cut the roots, pry the stump loose or pull it out with a chain connected to a winch.

removing shrubs

If you have a lot of shrubs to remove, rent or hire a backhoe or compact skid steer loader. Either one will make short work of the task.

If you want to keep some of the shrubs or smaller trees for transplanting, dig them out and wrap root balls in burlap individually. Maintain them until you're ready to plant by burying the root balls in wet sawdust or wood chips. Keep the root balls moist at all times.

HOW TO GET RID OF DEBRIS

When you have a lot of brush and tree limbs to dispose of, rent a chipping machine or call a tree-trimming company to do the chipping for you. The benefit of this approach is that it provides you with mulch.

Another solution is to call for a debris box. Debris boxes come in a variety of sizes, measured in cubic yards. To give you an idea of size, a 20-yard box is large enough to hold a midsize car.

If you are removing dirt, rocks, or broken concrete, ask for a debris box specifically designed to hold these materials. It is smaller than other debris boxes because it will hold a much heavier load. Debris-box companies can give you rental and size details particular to your area; check the Yellow Pages.

Be sure to ask whether you pay by volume or weight, and to specify exactly where you want the box placed. Otherwise the driver will leave it where it is most convenient to drop. And keep in mind that these boxes are heavy and can damage driveways and lawns.

protecting valued trees

Construction machinery operated in tight quarters may not only damage a tree but also compact the earth over its roots, which can sharply restrict water from reaching them.

To protect a tree, fence off an area around it that's as wide as the tree's drip line—the imaginary line around the tree beneath its outermost branches—and a few feet beyond if possible. Define the area that heavy equipment should avoid with fence posts and orange plastic fencing (below). If this leaves no room for the equipment to maneuver, spread 3 or 4 inches of wood chips around the tree and lay sheets of ½-inch plywood over the chips to disperse the vehicle's weight. You can protect the tree trunk by tying 2 by 4s around it.

In some cases, earth must be cut away close to trees, damaging their roots. Healthy trees can lose some roots and survive, but that's not true of old or unhealthy ones. If you must excavate near trees, cut larger

Use a tree well to protect an existing tree from a grade change.

new grade

new retaining wall

existing grade

exposed roots with a saw or loppers. Do not cut them with an ax or allow a trencher or backhoe to rip through them. To compensate for lost roots over the next few years, water the tree during droughts and keep it well mulched.

If soil compaction around a favorite tree is inevitable or has already occurred, you can relieve root suffocation by renting a soil auger. Drill holes about 3 inches in diameter and a foot apart, from the trunk to the drip line (or slightly beyond), and fill them with compost or mulch mixed with a root-promoting fertilizer. Water and air will then be able to percolate down through these holes and spread to the roots beneath the compacted areas.

Place fencing around the drip line of trees you're keeping to prevent machinery from compacting the root zone.

building a tree well

Sometimes the grade must be altered around a tree to protect it. This may involve adding soil above grade, removing some below it, or adding a retaining wall. It's acceptable to add about 4 inches of soil over existing ground around an established tree, because new roots can grow into this area. But if more than 4 inches of soil is required, a tree well, or level area partially encircled by a retaining wall, is needed before the grade change to prevent suffocation of the tree roots (see illustration, opposite page). A retaining wall can also be built below the tree to protect it when grade must be reduced on the downslope side. The well should be slightly wider than the tree's drip line and wider still around younger trees to allow for continued growth.

protecting a lawn and shrubs

If workmen must take wheelbarrows back and forth across a good lawn, lay down old boards or strips of plywood to keep the wheelbarrow tires from denting the sod. When heavy equipment must be driven across a lawn or sidewalk, make sure in advance that it has rubber tires or tracks, not metal tracks. Use ½-inch plywood sheets to distribute the weight. Protect fragile shrubs by fencing them off and then covering them with old sheets. If you use

Roger Cook measures exact elevations by sighting through a transit or builder's level at a vertical measuring pole.

plastic sheeting, be careful that the plants don't cook under it.

establishing rough grade

Rough grading ensures that water drains away from the house foundation and shapes the land to make it more useful or more interesting.

The basis of rough grading is cutting and filling: taking dirt from where it is not needed to where it can be used to reshape the terrain. But before you begin, check with your building department on wetlands restrictions and other grading regulations that affect your site. Also check to see if a permit is required.

How a site is graded depends on the project's size and complexity. If the project is just a pathway or new flowerbed, a wheelbarrow and shovel, combined with a 4-foot level on a straight piece of lumber, will do. Larger and more complex projects— usually undertaken by a grading contractor—may require heavy equipment, the use of a 100-foot tape measure, and an optical builder's level or transit to determine precise levels. (Laser levels are also fine—they're often not quite as precise, but simple to operate.)

Where rough grading will remove significant amounts of topsoil, you will need to decide what to do with the excess soil. Stockpiling topsoil consumes a lot of space, and much of the soil will dissipate unless protected under plastic tarps. This is why Roger Cook recommends that you haul soil away as soon as it's produced. By the same token, if you need to add topsoil, arrange for its delivery at the last possible moment and put it where you need it right away.

Even if you bring in a grading contractor to do the rough grading, the landscape contractor normally directs the finish grading, which involves placing, tilling, and smoothing out new topsoil.

subsurface drainage

In many yards, surface drainage is insufficient, and relandscaping requires that all or part of the drainage system be either updated or readdressed. If that's the case, you'll need to correct the problems with additional grading during the landscaping phase or by adding subsurface drains.

WAYS TO MANAGE WATER MOVEMENT AND DRAINAGE

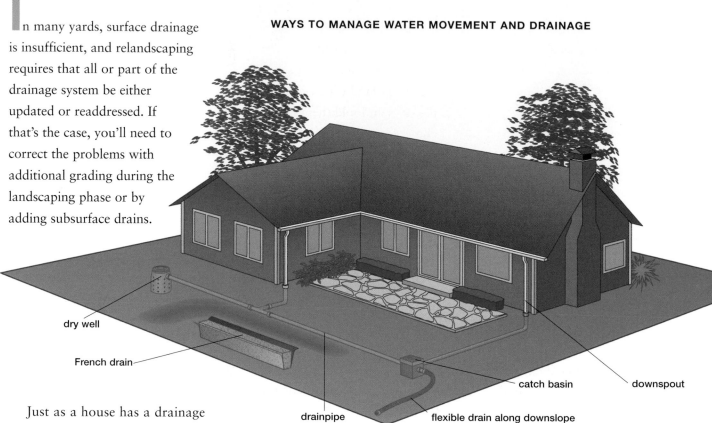

dry well

French drain

drainpipe

flexible drain along downslope

catch basin

downspout

Just as a house has a drainage system, yards that are slightly lower than surrounding properties, or that have high water tables or water-collecting low spots, will have to have their own array of inlets, outlets, pipes, and basins to catch and redirect water on and below grade. While rough and finish grading will help keep surface water away from the house, subsurface drains are often required to handle larger amounts of water.

One of the biggest sources of excess water in a landscape is the water that gutters and downspouts funnel from the roof to the immediate area around the house. Unless that water is redirected, it will eventually flow into the crawl space or basement, which can set off a host of water-related problems.

The illustration above shows some of the strategies used in subsurface drainage networks. Water from downspouts is directed to underground drain lines; water that puddles in a low spot in the lawn is collected and drained. It can be diverted to a dry well or a French drain; both help speed its absorption by the earth. Most water goes to a catch basin that allows debris to sink to the bottom while the water keeps moving.

If you plan to build a patio or deck beside your house, it's a good idea to install a drainpipe beneath the area first, particularly if there will be a downspout nearby. That way, rainwater will readily flow away from the area rather than flood it.

French drains

Also called curtain drains, French drains are ditches installed in a low area that would otherwise allow water to pond. Water is held until it

BASIC FRENCH DRAIN

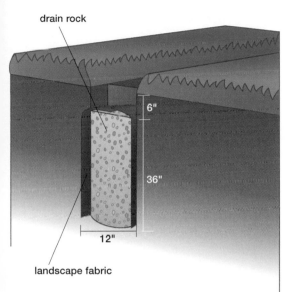

drain rock

6"

36"

12"

landscape fabric

percolates into the surrounding soil. French drains are particularly useful where dense or compacted soil layers slow water drainage.

A French drain is commonly dug about a foot wide and 3 to 4 feet deep. Its length depends on the soil and the amount of anticipated water. Hire a landscape contractor or soil engineer to help with the calculations. If considerable water collects, two or more French drains can be installed parallel to each other, about 4 feet apart.

To install a French drain under a lawn, carefully remove the turf and set it aside so it can be reinstalled later. Make cleanup easier by placing plastic sheeting on both sides of the

ditch, one side for the soil and the other for the sod.

After the ditch is dug, drape lengths of landscape cloth down the sides and fold them back about 8 inches over the outside edge. It is not necessary to cover the bottom of the ditch, but make sure the cloth laps over the edges of the ditch. This will prevent silt from washing in among the drain rock and rendering the drain useless.

Fill the trench with washed drain rock 2 to 3 inches in diameter (see Ordering Drain Rock at right). The more space between the rocks to hold excess water until it percolates into the soil, the better. Fill the ditch to within 6 inches of the top and then fold the landscape cloth over the rock to keep sediment out. Fill the remainder of the ditch with soil, tamp it thoroughly, and then replace the sod. If your French drain is in an area not covered by lawn, fill the trench to the top with rock.

A French drain wrapped in landscape fabric has a life span of 5 to 10 years. By that time, the layer of rock will fill with soil that has worked its way past the fabric. Without the fabric, the rock layer will silt up faster and the useful life span will be half as long.

ORDERING DRAIN ROCK

No national standard specifies sizes of rock, and rock goes by different names in different states. In some areas, rock 1½ to 2 inches in diameter is known as medium-sized cobblestone, while gravel contractors in other areas have no idea what cobblestone is. The best way to order drain rock is to call a local sand and gravel dealer and ask for round rock about 2 inches in diameter for a French drain or curtain drain system. Round rocks allow more space between them than crushed or broken rock, resulting in better percolation. Be sure to stipulate that you want washed rock, which is exactly that. Otherwise, you may receive rock covered with sand, which is commonly delivered for concrete work.

piped drains

If water flows toward the house or forms a pond in your yard during rainstorms, you may need to install perforated pipe in gravel-filled ditches to remove it. This is often the case if your house is in a low spot, at the base of a hill, or on particularly flat ground. In such situations, drains must be sloped to carry water to a city storm-drain system or to a near-by natural-drainage system, such as a creek or marsh. Keep in mind that any work within 100 feet of a creek or wetland may be prohibited, and city approval is usually required before you connect to a storm drain.

How deep a drainage trench should be depends on the location. When placed around a foundation to keep water away from a basement or crawl space, the trench should extend to the bottom of the footing to be effective. Any trench deeper than 5 feet must, by code, have an approved means of exit at both ends and be shored to prevent possible collapse during the digging and installation process (local codes may vary). Shoring deep ditches is a job best left to the professionals. It involves placing heavy sheets of plywood or steel on the vertical trench sides and holding them in place with 2 by 4s or adjustable metal spreaders while work is in progress. When the job is finished, the plywood and spreaders are removed and the trench is backfilled.

No matter how deep the trench, line it with landscape cloth, add about 3 inches of crushed rock, and begin laying in the 4-inch-diameter perforated PVC drainpipe. Only a portion of the pipe's circumference is perforated; set the drain holes up to collect water from above and pipe it away; position holes down where the water table is high so that some water can leach into the soil.

To ensure that water flows, set perforated drainpipe in the trench at a slope of approximately 1 inch for every 10 feet of run. Place a 4-foot level on top of the pipe with a ⅜-inch-thick block of wood under the lower end. When the bubble is centered, the slope is just right. You can also use a builder's level, transit, or a laser level and tape measure to check the pipe's slope.

SLOPING PERFORATED PIPE

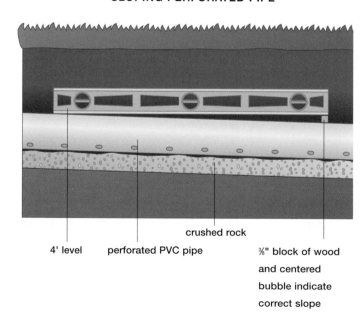

4' level perforated PVC pipe

crushed rock

⅜" block of wood and centered bubble indicate correct slope

INSTALLING PERFORATED PIPE DRAIN

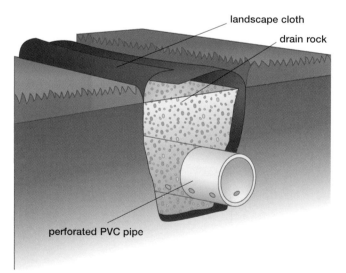

landscape cloth

drain rock

perforated PVC pipe

Perforated pipe collects water and either speeds its movement away (holes facing up) or also allows some absorption by soil (holes facing down). Placing holes at the bottom also drains soil plagued by a rising water table more quickly.

As each pipe segment is put in place, confirm that the degree of drop is maintained, then backfill with crushed rock and fold the landscape cloth over it. This will keep sediment from clogging the pipe. Then cover the surface with sod or decorative gravel.

drainage destinations

Water that is directed away from a house has to go somewhere, but often the place is not obvious. In some cases, you can direct water to storm drains, in others to natural-terrain runoffs as long as this does not interfere with local regulations. In desert climates where rainfall is minimal and much needed, you may want to collect drainage water in a cistern for later use. A classic solution, useful in most regions, is a dry well.

Dry wells are similar to French drains, but excess water is usually piped from another location to it. Dry wells are commonly just round holes about 4 feet deep that are filled with rocks. But Roger Cook notes that sooner or later, silt will permeate the spaces

tip: solid pipes In areas where drainpipe passes close to trees, use solid instead of perforated pipe to prevent tree roots from growing through the holes and plugging the pipe.

between the rocks, rendering the well useless. Instead, Roger prefers a large manufactured dry well—basically a plastic container with numerous holes in it. When silt becomes excessive, open the container and clean it out.

The container can be anything from a 55 gallon plastic drum to a 1,000-gallon concrete cistern. Fiberglass septic tanks, which range from 500 to 1,200 gallons, also work well. Water will percolate out through holes that must be drilled in any of these containers. Wrap the dry well in landscape cloth before backfilling around it to reduce silt penetration.

Locate dry wells away from the water problem area, using a shallow drainage trench to carry the water from the problem area to the dry well.

DRY WELL

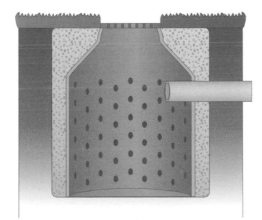

Like French drains, dry wells collect water in an area where the surrounding soil can slowly absorb it.

CATCH BASIN

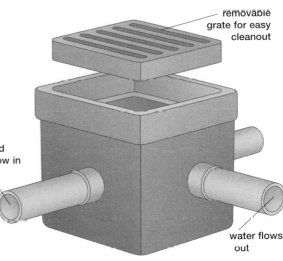

removable grate for easy cleanout

water and debris flow in

water flows out

Water moves into a catch basin from multiple directions, and out one direction.

Catch basins are designed to collect water from various sources and send it in only one direction. Catch basins also trap leaves, pine needles, and other debris that tends to be washed along during rainy weather.

The catch basin is simply a box, which can be as small as 4 inches but is usually much larger, with one or more inlet pipes and an attached outlet pipe. When water runs into the basin, any debris carried along with it eventually sinks to the bottom; the water keeps on flowing.

Catch basins are always installed with an accessible top grate so they can be cleaned periodically. Leaves and other debris can be removed by hand or with a wet/dry shop vacuum.

planning water systems

Having a complete watering system for the lawn and garden means more than not having to drag hoses around anymore. Sprinklers or drip irrigation—or both—ensure that your lawn and plants will be watered as often and in the right volume with less wasted water.

There are a few steps to take before you choose a watering system. The planning process includes making a scale drawing or map of areas to be irrigated, determining the water pressure and how much water is available on a sustained basis, and then deciding which of your garden areas are best watered with sprinklers, with drip, or both. This section (pages 74–81) will outline the basic steps, but be sure to read detailed planning guides found at home improvement centers or irrigation-supply dealers before you begin work (see the Resource Guide on page 184).

make a landscape map

A scale drawing of the areas to be watered, the hydrozone, is essential. The drawing will help you plan the piping layout in the most economical and efficient manner, and let you determine the size and coverage areas of the sprinklers or drip emitters.

Using graph paper, make a scale drawing of your property on which

Pop-up sprinkler systems for lawns are convenient and improve growth.

each square equals 1 foot. Measure the outer perimeter of the lot first and draw it to scale on your map. (If you already developed a base map as described on page 18, start with that.) Then draw in the house, pathways, driveway, and any other structures. Now draw in trees, including their approximate drip lines, and any shrubs, vegetable gardens, and flowerbeds. Finally, draw in the lawn area.

From the map, identify areas that will need automatic watering and calculate the length and width of each hydrozone. Each requires a watering plan designed for its specific needs.

flow rates and pressure

To design and plan your watering system, you need to know the water pressure and how many gallons of water are available to your home on a sustained basis. Residences on municipal water systems usually have about 30 or 50 pounds per square inch (psi) of water pressure and 10 gallons per minute (gpm) of flow, exactly what most sprinkler systems are designed for. But water supply can vary from home to home, so be sure to measure your own water capacity before designing.

Water pressure is important because if the pressure is too low, the spray won't cover the intended area. If it is too high (over 80 psi) you'll need to reduce it by installing a pressure regulator.

The easiest way to determine the water flow and pressure at the same time is with a combination flow and pressure gauge. This device threads onto any hose bib, but choose the one nearest the house's water supply for greatest accuracy. The device will accurately measure flow up to 13 gpm and pressure up to 160 psi.

If you have trouble finding a combination gauge, measure the pressure with a common pressure gauge, and directly measure the flow rate by timing how fast the spigot fills a 5-gallon bucket. Again, start with the hose bib nearest your main water supply line. Open the valve completely and time to the second how long it takes to fill the container. Then divide 60 (seconds) by the number of seconds it took to fill, and multiply that by the size of the bucket. For example, if it took 25 seconds to fill a 5-gallon bucket, the math would be 60 ÷ 25 × 5 = 12, or 12 gpm.

Flow rates are important when you are planning drip systems too, only the standard measure is gallons per hour instead of gallons per minute. Multiply the gpm available by 60 to see how many gallons of water are delivered per hour.

Once you've determined the amount, you can figure out how many sprinklers can be operated at one time. If the water volume is high, you can operate more sprinklers at once than if the volume is low.

circuits and valves

Because residential water pressure is generally insufficient to power sprinklers for an entire yard at the same time, and because you'll likely want to water some areas more than others, watering systems are divided into individual circuits, each of which is controlled by one manual or electric valve.

Manual valves need to be turned on or off; electric valves are turned on and off by a controller, which is a clock that includes one or more programmable watering schedules.

timers and sensors

Timers allow you to set the days, hour, and length of time for each valve to operate. But nothing is worse than watching sprinklers come on during a heavy downpour, or wasting water on soil that is already moist. Rain or soil-moisture sensors override the set program when either of those conditions prevails. Many new timers are sensor-ready and make the connections simple with one or two wire terminals. But even lacking that, wiring is not complicated. Check with manufacturers for details.

A TYPICAL AUTOMATIC SPRINKLER SYSTEM

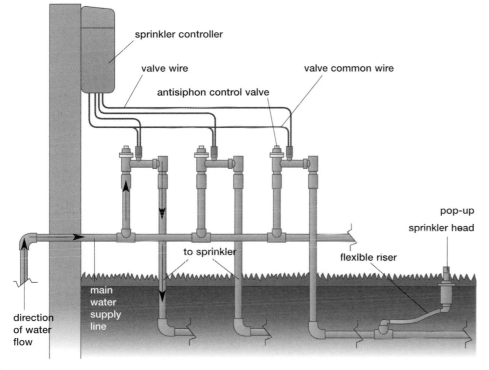

SPRINKLERS OR DRIP?

Sprinklers use more water and use it less efficiently than drip irrigation, but sprinklers can cover much larger areas. With a wide variety of sizes and adjustable spray patterns, sprinklers are ideal for lawns or thickly planted flowerbeds. But when you want to deliver water in precise amounts to specific locations, such as trees, shrubs, ground covers, or rows of vegetables, drip-irrigation systems are perfect. Both sprinklers and drip watering systems can be connected to controllers and sensors to ensure that your plants are watered even when you are away.

underground sprinklers

Now that you have a plan of your yard noting the different areas you need to water, and you know what your water pressure and volume are, the next step is to determine which type of sprinklers you will need. Take your plan to an irrigation-supply dealer or the irrigation department of a home improvement center for information and literature on sprinkler choices, spacing, and gallons used.

There are three basic types of sprinklers: fixed spray, geared rotary (quiet), and impact-rotary (noisy). All are available in versions that sit at a fixed height or that pop up to operate, then retract below ground for both safety and aesthetics. Each sprinkler includes information on the gallons of water used per minute and the throw distance of the water.

Fixed sprays come with full-, half-, and quarter-spray nozzles that cover from 5 to 15 feet and cost $3 to $5 each. Rotary sprinklers throw water from 15 to 50 feet, depending upon the model, which can reduce trenching and the number of valves and sprinklers needed to water large areas. These sprinklers cost $15 to $25 each.

Keep in mind that water from each sprinkler head should reach all adjacent heads. For example, if you're using a sprinkler with a radius of 15 feet, place sprinklers no more than 15 feet apart. In windy areas, compensate by placing sprinklers closer, in this example no more than 12 feet apart.

connect to the water supply

One of the easiest ways to connect a sprinkler system is to attach it to an outside faucet, or hose bib. You can also tap into your water line as it emerges from the front-yard water meter or in the basement (left).

TYPICAL BASEMENT SPRINKLER CONNECTION FOR COLD CLIMATES

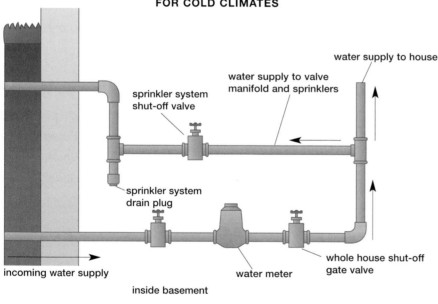

water supply to house

water supply to valve manifold and sprinklers

sprinkler system shut-off valve

sprinkler system drain plug

incoming water supply

inside basement

water meter

whole house shut-off gate valve

HOW TO CUT, PRIME, AND GLUE PVC PIPE

You can readily cut PVC pipe with a hacksaw or a special PVC cutter. When using a hacksaw, smooth the cut edges with sandpaper. The PVC cutter (right) is faster and leaves smooth edges. To connect pipes, first wipe both the outside and inside of the fitting and the pipe end with a clean cloth, then swab both with primer. This cleans and softens the PVC surface. Swab both areas with glue and then push the pipe and the fitting together with a slight twist. The glue sets in seconds. If you make a mistake, cut the pipe and use a coupler to reconnect it.

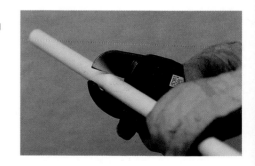

sprinkler manifold

This is where the main water supply connects to the individual circuits. Mount it in a convenient location and connect it to the water line with T fittings. Be sure there is a gate valve downstream of the manifold so that irrigation lines can be shut off without shutting off water to the house.

antisiphon device

All sprinkler systems need some kind of backflow device that prevents water from the yard from contaminating the house water supply. Required by plumbing codes, these are always installed about 12 inches above grade (or above the highest sprinkler). Most residential systems use valves with an integral antisiphon device. Larger sprinkler systems may utilize a pressure vacuum breaker.

control valves

Each valve controls one watering circuit. Valves with an integral antisiphon device are designed to be installed above ground, while in-line valves are installed below grade in systems protected by a pressure vacuum breaker.

trenches

Before you start to dig, check with your utility company to determine if there are any underground gas, electric, or water lines (see page 66). Make the ditch about 9 inches deep. For easy cleanup, put down plastic sheeting on both sides of the ditch, one for sod, one for soil

assembling and draining the system

Double-check your plan measurements and mark the location for each sprinkler. Then, starting from the antisiphon valve in each zone, begin connecting the pipe. PVC pipe is preferred wherever soil doesn't freeze. Polyethylene pipe is preferred where it does. Either is light and flexible, so you can cut and connect it beside the ditch and drop it right in.

At the spot where each riser will be located, screw the riser temporarily into a T. Use a level to ensure the riser is vertical as you glue the T in place. Then, after all connections are made, wrap Teflon tape over the riser threads and screw the risers permanently into the Ts. When all risers are installed, turn on each circuit for a few minutes to blow out any dirt. Now cut the risers to the exact height for the sprinklers and attach the sprinklers. If the sprinklers are to be flush with a lawn, use flexible pipe risers so that you can set the final height precisely.

After checking that all valves and sprinklers are operating properly and there are no leaks, backfill the trenches without pushing risers out of plumb. Water the trenches thoroughly to settle the soil, then add more soil as needed until the sprinklers are flush with the ground.

If you live in a cold-winter climate, sprinkler lines must be emptied before soil freezes. Systems can be designed with manual or automatic drain valves, or you can winterize by blowing water out with compressed air. Do it yourself (a 100 cfm compressor is usually sufficient), or check with a landscape or irrigation contractor.

Flexible risers make accurate positioning of sprinklers much easier.

drip irrigation

With the increasing need for water conservation in recent years, drip irrigation has continued to grow in popularity. In addition to saving water, drip irrigation benefits plant growth and reduces the numbers of weeds. Drip systems come in myriad configurations, so generalization is difficult. But don't assume these systems require a lot of fussing. Modern emitters are more reliable than earlier versions, and much less likely to plug.

Drip irrigation provides water slowly and steadily to exact areas through a series of small tubes with the appropriate watering device on the end to control the water flow. It is excellent for flowerbeds, vegetable gardens, and long rows of shrubs or large planter boxes. It is also particularly useful for hillside plantings where sprinkler water tends to run off.

Different emitters deliver different amounts of water in different ways, such as trickling, misting, and spraying. Systems typically connect directly to an outside faucet, along with a filter, a pressure regulator, and an antisiphon device. Drip irrigation often has what appears to be a confusing array of parts, but with careful

Position drip emitter over the plant's root ball. This one is held in place with a stake.

planning even a beginner will have little difficulty assembling them.

drip watering devices

There are four common kinds of drip watering devices.

■ *Emitters* literally drip, like the one pictured above.

■ *Misters* create a fine spray, usually over a single plant.

■ *Microsprays* cover larger areas but with a very low volume of water.

■ The *emitter line* is tubing with emitters built in every 12 or 18 inches.

valves

In a simple hookup, a filter and drip line are attached to an outside faucet, with feeder tubes extending from this line. This is the style shown on the bottom right of the opposite page. You can add a battery-operated combination valve and timer to enable automation at minimal expense.

In a more permanent (and automatic) arrangement, shown at the top of the opposite page, a separate supply line for drip irrigation includes a manifold and electric valve, just as for any permanent watering system.

pressure regulator

Drip-irrigation systems usually take only 10 to 30 psi of water pressure, much less than the 40 to 60 psi common in most household water systems. The pressure regulator is necessary to prevent the drip tubing from bursting.

filter

All drip-irrigation systems need a filter. Even city water contains some fine sediment that can eventually plug up emitters; well water needs a larger filter. Various types of filters are available, but screen filters are most widely used for residential systems. These filters are simple to remove and clean by rinsing.

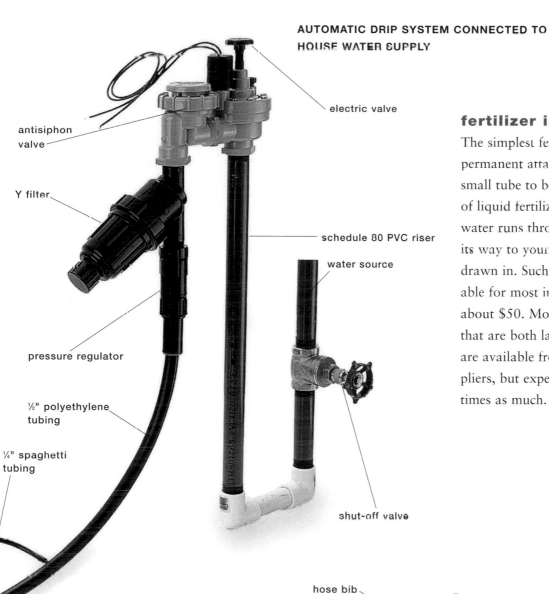

electric valve

antisiphon valve

Y filter

schedule 80 PVC riser

water source

pressure regulator

½" polyethylene tubing

¼" spaghetti tubing

shut-off valve

fertilizer injector

The simplest fertilizer injector is a permanent attachment that allows a small tube to be run from a container of liquid fertilizer to the system. As water runs through the drip line on its way to your plants, fertilizer is drawn in. Such a basic setup is suitable for most installations and costs about $50. More elaborate injectors that are both larger and more precise are available from drip-system suppliers, but expect to pay at least three times as much.

**MANUAL DRIP SYSTEM
CONNECTED TO A HOSE BIB**

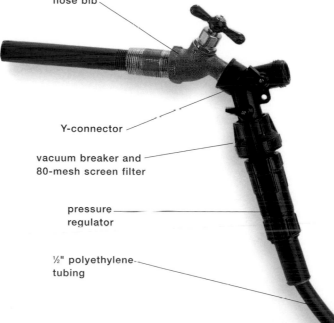

hose bib

Y-connector

vacuum breaker and 80-mesh screen filter

pressure regulator

½" polyethylene tubing

planning the system

Just as for all sprinklers, plan drip systems around separate circuits that deliver water to plants with similar needs. Where drip systems differ is in their precision, giving individual plants what they need and wasting less to evaporation, weeds, or runoff.

Some points to consider in planning circuits are:

■ Separate plants that need the most water from those that need the least into separate circuits if possible. When it's not, add extra emitters around plants that need more water.

■ Sandy soil may need higher flow rates than heavier loam or clay soils. If water puddles around a plant, reduce the flow rate, or cycle two shorter waterings with a gap between them.

■ Water larger, deep-rooted trees and shrubs less often but for a longer time than annuals and flowerbeds.

As with a sprinkler system, you'll need a scale drawing of your property showing all the areas to be watered. Then you need to determine the flow rate and water pressure (see page 74). But remember that drip devices are rated in gallons per hour. If your water supply provides 10 gpm, that is equivalent to 600 gallons per hour (10 gpm × 60 minutes per hour).

When you begin selecting the emitters, you'll be choosing between output rates of $\frac{1}{2}$ gallon, 1 gallon, or 2 gallons per hour. The total output for any one circuit should not exceed 75 percent of the water volume available.

Starting from the water source, also measure the different runs through the garden. The total run distance of any one circuit should not exceed 400 feet, because water friction in the pipe causes uneven flow.

Main pipe runs between the water source and the valves. If you must deliver water long distances, run a $\frac{3}{4}$- to 1-inch PVC pipe underground to the area, install a riser and hose bib, and then install the valves and antisiphon device there.

Lateral lines carry water from the valves to the area to be watered. This pipe is commonly $\frac{1}{2}$- or $\frac{5}{8}$-inch flexible polyethylene tubing. Branch lines, emitters, and microtubing can all be attached to it.

Spaghetti tubing, or microtubing, is $\frac{1}{4}$-inch-diameter solid vinyl tubing designed to carry water to plants some distance from the lateral line.

A TYPICAL DRIP IRRIGATION PLAN

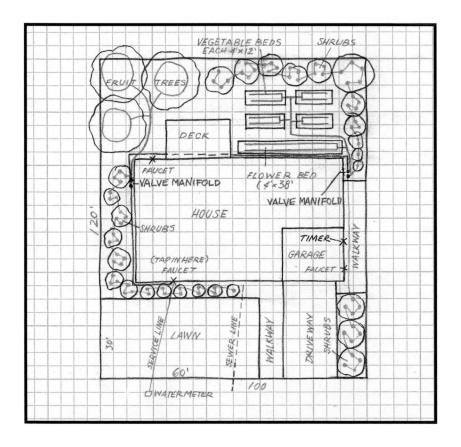

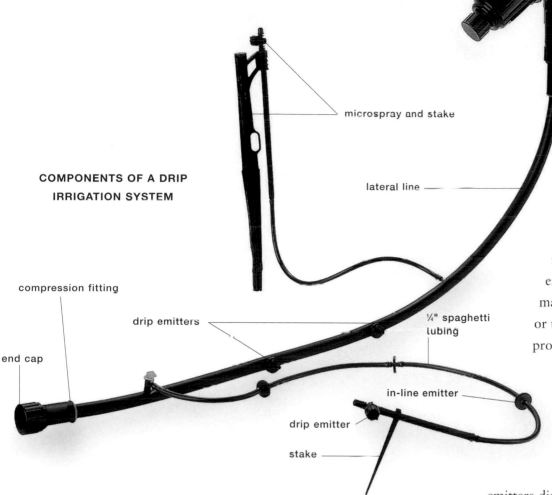

COMPONENTS OF A DRIP IRRIGATION SYSTEM

microspray and stake

lateral line

compression fitting

drip emitters

¼" spaghetti tubing

end cap

in-line emitter

drip emitter

stake

From the lateral line for each zone, add branch lines as needed. Then extend the drip tubes and appropriate emitters to each plant. Do not exceed the manufacturer's recommendations for maximum drip-tube length, or the plant may not get the proper amount of water.

Many experts recommend putting two emitters opposite each other by a small plant and four around shrubs and trees. The additional drip emitters disperse water more equally.

To reduce waterborne disease and ensure water gets to roots, Roger Cook advises that emitters be kept back a little from the plant stem so the water goes directly down to the root ball. On more established plants, this may be 2 to 3 feet back from the stem.

Use special plastic or wire stakes to hold tubing lightly in place every 3 feet or so to ensure emitters stay put. Tubing doesn't need to be buried, but covering it with mulch makes the garden more attractive.

Connectors are the elbows, couplers, and Ts that you need to join drip systems together. Compression fittings are pressed over the tubing by "walking" (rocking) the fitting onto the tubing, while barbed fittings are pushed over the tubing. Be sure to match the fittings you buy to the size of tubing you're using.

Electric timers are an essential part of the time- and water-saving value of drip systems. You can use the same timers for drip that you would for sprinklers, and if the timer offers more than one program, you can control drip circuits with one program and spray circuits with another.

(They require different programs, as the drip circuit will need to operate on a different schedule.)

No wiring or plumbing is required to set up a simple, battery-powered timer (below) to operate one valve. These connect directly to a hose bib and set up in minutes.

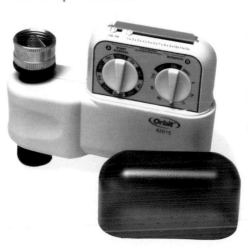

Battery-powered timers are the easiest way to automate a simple drip system.

landscape edging

An attractive edging can make the difference between an ordinary landscaping project and an outstanding one. Edging may be used to define one particular area or to separate adjoining spaces, such as a lawn from a flowerbed. Some edging, like flexible plastic, is nearly invisible, while other types are bolder, such as brick or cobblestone.

When selecting edging, consider whether to place it flush with the ground or raised. Around lawns, flush edging allows you to mow over it rather than trim around it. But raised edging better highlights the area it surrounds, which is often the objective.

selecting edging materials

Before choosing a material, consider whether you want your edging to make a statement, simply be utilitarian, or not be noticed at all. Following are some of the most widely used edging materials.

Brick is one of the most traditional and versatile edgings and can be laid in sand or mortar. Bricks can be installed flat or on edge, end to end, or side by side. They come in a wide range of colors and sizes, but for landscaping purposes, always select

those marked SX, which indicates they're capable of withstanding severe weathering.

Wood, treated or naturally decay-resistant 1-bys, goes with many landscape styles and can be made to curve. Hold the boards in place with wood stakes driven into the ground on the outside of the curve and screw through the board into the stake. To curve a board, make a series of cuts, called kerfs, at least half way through the board on the inside of the curve. Space the kerfs about 2 inches apart. Benderboard is ⅜-by-6-inch lumber often cut from redwood that serve well for informal edging along curving borders or pathways. Most popular in the West, they are thin enough to bend easily without kerfing.

Composite wood edging is quick to install and creates a tidy border between mulched bed and lawn.

Plastic and composite wood boards have become increasingly popular as edging materials. Both are highly resistant to rot and flexible enough to bend around curves without being kerfed. Once bent into position, they tend to hold their shape without immediately springing back, which makes them easier than wood to install. They are most often used as deck planking and sold for that purpose in ¾-by-6 pieces.

Composites (made of recycled plastic and wood fiber), are sold by brands such as Trex and SmartDeck, and come in 1-by-4, 2-by-4, 1-by-6, and ¾-by-6 dimensions, and in brown and tan.

Timbers, whether pressure-treated or decay-resistant redwood or cedar, are effective and easy to install; so much so that the look has become a bit tired. These 4-by-4 or 4-by-6 posts can be dug in so they're flush with the ground, or laid on the ground and staked in place to form a raised perimeter. Avoid using old railroad ties, as they contain toxic creosote.

Plastic and metal edging can be curved and staked to provide an easy-

Install flexible plastic edging by opening a trench; secure with matching plastic stakes.

to-install rigid border for walkways (below, left). Dig a shallow, narrow trench, place the plastic edging into the ditch, and stake in place about every 3 feet. Fill the remainder of the trench with crushed rock, and then place cut rock or pavers along the outside to hide the edging.

Stone is a virtually indestructible edging. Choose from cobblestone, field rubble, river rock, flat lengths of limestone, or pieces of warmly colored flagstone set on edge. Partially bury cut stone in the earth for a natural look.

Precast concrete is an inexpensive edging made in short sections; it's available curved, straight, and with scalloped tops. Although easily installed, it's not very distinctive in appearance. Clear a shallow trench, place the edging in, and backfill.

Small boulders serve the dual purpose of edging a path and holding back surrounding earth and vegetation.

MORTARED BRICK BORDER

A mortared brick border lends a nice formality to a path or flower- bed, and it's rock solid. Begin by digging a footing ditch just narrower than the brick is long. The ditch should be 4 inches deep in areas where the soil does not freeze, but below the frost level in colder areas. Fill the ditch with concrete to ground level and smooth it with a trowel. (This process works equally well if the ditch follows contours up and down the border area.) After the concrete cures for a day or two, spread a ½-inch layer of mortar on the footing and place bricks in it side by side. Space the bricks ⅜ inch apart with scraps of plywood. After the mortar cures for a day, use a grout bag to fill the spaces between the bricks with mortar. For a narrower edging that uses fewer bricks, place them end to end.

landscape lighting

Outdoor lighting makes your yard as enjoyable at night as it is during the day, or even more so. Night lighting not only enhances your property's appearance but can also improve security and safety. Timers on the system's transformer will switch the lights on and off at preset times or simply on at dusk and off at daybreak.

lighting systems

Of all the outdoor lighting systems available, the low-voltage system is the least expensive and most practical; plus you can install it yourself. Your other choice is to have 120-volt wiring extended from the house, which requires a licensed electrician.

To develop a lighting plan, divide your garden into three zones: a foreground with midlevel brightness; a middle ground with low-level lights that create shadows; and a background that is brightly lit in order to draw the eye through the garden.

Discreet outdoor lights gently illuminate an entry path, guiding the way to the front door.

low-voltage components

Low-voltage systems are controlled by a transformer, which is plugged into a standard 120-volt exterior outlet and reduces the current to a harmless 12 volts. Transformers typically handle from 50 watts to 1,000 watts or more and have two or more circuits. To match a transformer to your needs, add up the number of watts that all the bulbs in your design will use, then pick a transformer that will handle at least 50 percent more. This allows you to readily expand later.

In its simplest form, low-voltage outdoor lighting can be purchased in a kit that typically includes 6 to 12 lights, the wire, and the transformer. For a more versatile and better-quality system, purchase the items individually.

Kits commonly come with 14-gauge wires, which are sufficient for 200 watts or less, but use 12-gauge wire for more than 200 watts. Larger wire (the lower the gauge number, the larger the wire) helps prevent voltage loss that results in dim lights at the end of the run.

A typical arrangement of lights and wiring for an outdoor system.

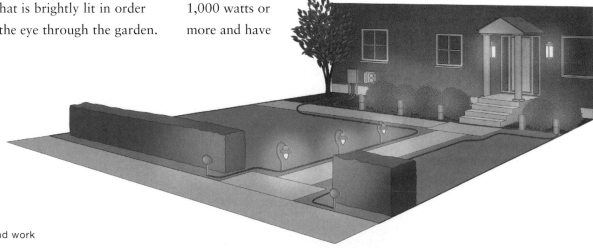

Lamp materials range from low-end plastics to high-quality copper or brass. Many lamps are mounted on stakes and pushed into the ground. Bulbs range from 10 to 100 watts or more, with the most common range between 20 and 50 watts. For bulbs, choose between incandescent, which last 600 to 1,000 hours, and the significantly brighter but more expensive halogen, which last 1,000 to 4,000 hours.

installing low-voltage landscape lighting

3 At the transformer, use wire strippers to remove ½ inch of insulation from the ends of two wires. Insert the stripped ends under the two terminal screws on the transformer and tighten the screws. In some cases, you may have to bend the wires in a tight loop to fit around the terminal screw. Plug the transformer into a nearby outlet. If the transformer and outlet are located outdoors, the outlet must be protected by a ground fault circuit interrupter (GFCI), and the outlet box must be weatherproof.

2 When running wire to lamps beside a sidewalk, the wire needs to be hidden. To do this, use a square-tipped shovel to remove a 12-inch-wide section of lawn beside the walk and fold it back. With the shovel, scratch a 3-inch-deep ditch in the soil for the wire. Fold the sod back in place, but as you do, make a slit in it at each lamp location and pull a loop of the wire through.

Alternatively, push a spade 4 inches deep in a line across the lawn. As you go, widen each slit by pushing the shovel handle forward. Use a stick to push the wire down into the slit, leaving a loop on the surface for each lamp. Finally, press the sod together with your foot.

1 Place the lamps for each circuit on the ground at their locations and then run the wire beside them. Low-voltage wire is designed to lie on the surface or be buried. In some areas it can be hidden among plants or under ground cover. Where wires cross lawns, they should be buried.

4 After positioning all the lamps on the circuit, begin making the electrical connections while the transformer is on; this will confirm that each lamp is working. (The low voltage poses no danger.) Most low-voltage systems use needle-style clamps to make the connections. Open the connector hanging from the bottom of each lamp and slip it over the wire. Press the connector together firmly until it clicks into place. The tiny needles penetrate the insulation and touch the wires inside to make the electrical connection. If the lamp does not light, reposition the connector and try again, or check the bulb.

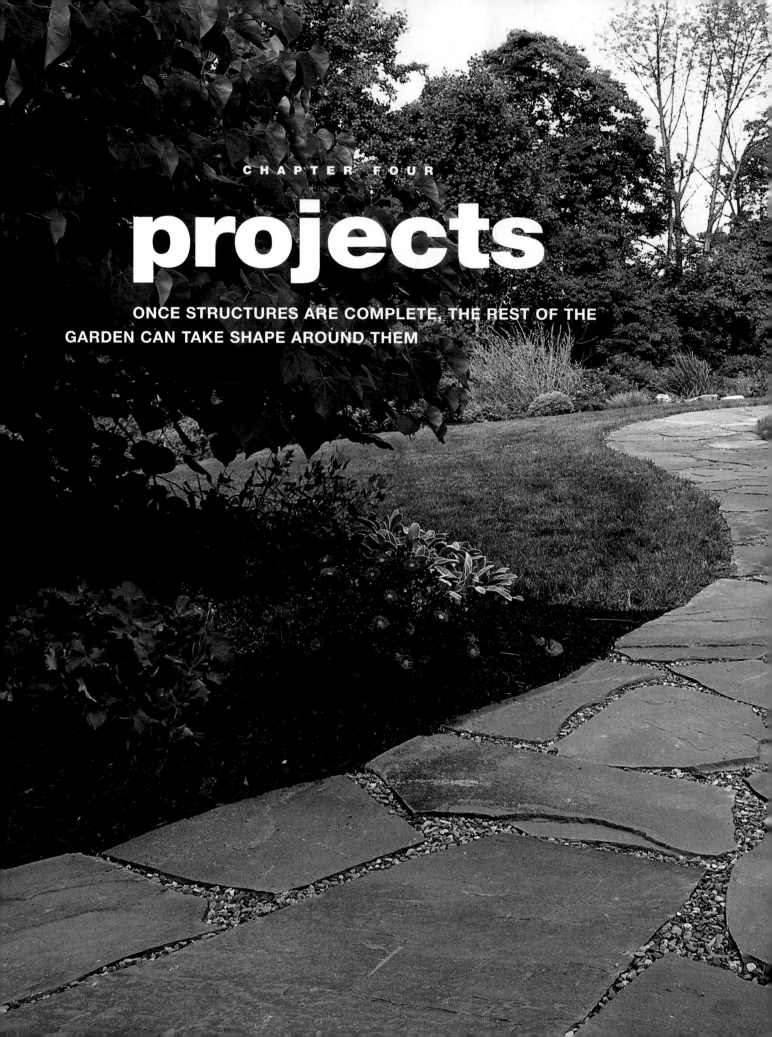

projects

ONCE STRUCTURES ARE COMPLETE, THE REST OF THE GARDEN CAN TAKE SHAPE AROUND THEM

OUTDOOR STRUCTURES LIKE THE ONES IN THIS CHAPTER give a garden shape and character. They also tend to be the costliest part of your landscaping effort, which is one reason providing your own labor makes sense.

If you're an old hand at outdoor building projects, you may be able to proceed without a lot of help. But many homeowners will benefit from seeing how the experts do it, which is what this chapter is about. Included are 11 projects—some simple, some complex—from paths and steps to walls and water features.

While it's unlikely that every detail of these projects will apply to your situation, seeing the full range of design considerations, material choices, and building procedures will give you an excellent foundation for taking on your own project. The key is investing the time to plan and think through the process, then leaving yourself plenty of time to complete the construction. However, be realistic about your own limitations and, if you need to, enlist some experienced help. Whether you do all the work or just some of it, you'll enjoy the results many times more for the effort you made.

brick path

Few landscape features are as attractive or as inviting as a brick pathway. Brick's warm color and rich texture harmonize with many garden styles and offer a pleasing contrast to the surrounding vegetation. And over time, as the bricks weather slightly, the path's lines will soften, making the walkway seem like a natural feature.

materials and tools

- 4-by-8-inch bricks (4½ bricks per square foot, plus 10 percent for waste)
- stone dust
- ¾-inch gravel
- 1-by-3 boards, standard grade or better (select for small knots)
- 1-by-2 stakes spaced 6 feet apart
- long hose to mark out the path
- 1⅝-inch galvanized decking screws
- 4-foot-long 2 by 4 for screed
- digging shovel
- square-nose shovel
- steel rake
- rubber mallet
- mason's hammer
- level
- push broom
- brick set (mason's chisel)
- cordless screwdriver
- radial-arm saw or slide-compound miter saw
- gas-powered plate compactor or hand tamper
- ear and eye protection (for cutting brick)
- masonry wet saw (optional)
- sod cutter (optional)

The handsome 4-foot-wide brick walkway shown here uses a combination of new, shiny, water-struck bricks and bricks salvaged from a 200-year-old building. The 4-by-8-inch bricks are laid in a classic basket-weave design and bordered on each side by a soldier course of vertical bricks.

To ensure that your walkway survives temperature extremes in cold climates, use only bricks designated as SX, for "severe weathering." These

Few landscape features are as attractive or as inviting as a brick pathway. Brick's warm color and rich texture harmonize with many garden styles and offer a pleasing contrast to the surrounding vegetation. And over time, as the bricks weather slightly, the path's lines will soften, making the walkway seem like a natural feature.

The handsome 4-foot-wide brick walkway shown here uses a combination of new, shiny, water-struck bricks and bricks salvaged from a 200-year-old building. The 4-by-8-inch bricks are laid in a classic basket-weave design and bordered on each side by a soldier course of vertical bricks.

To ensure that your walkway survives temperature extremes in cold climates, use only bricks designated as SX, for "severe weathering." These bricks are fired in the kiln for longer periods and at higher temperatures than standard bricks, so they're extremely hard and weather resistant. Elsewhere, MX ("moderate weathering") bricks can be used.

pathway options

There are two basic ways to build a brick path: either on a base of stone dust (or sand), or on a slab. Mortared pavement provides a flatter, more stable pathway, but it's also more difficult to build. First the path is excavated, then a base of gravel is added. The gravel is compacted and topped with a steel-reinforced slab of poured concrete. Once the concrete cures, a 1-inch-thick bed of mortar is troweled across the surface and the bricks are pressed into place. The spaces between the bricks are also filled with mortar.

Flexible pavement, commonly called the dry-laid method, consists of setting the bricks on a base of gravel and a bed of stone dust (composed of tiny stone slivers and dust). This is the quickest and least expensive technique because there's no concrete to pour or mortar to mix. The bricks can be butted tightly together or separated by about ¼ inch to create visible joints. Stone dust or sand

1 Once you've established one edge of the path, use a mallet to drive 1-by-2 stakes into the ground alongside the hose. Space the stakes about 6 feet apart, as shown. To define the opposite edge of the pathway, measure 4 feet (for a 4-foot-wide path) from each stake and drive its mate into the ground.

2 Remove the sod and several inches of soil from between the staked edges of the path. For this task, consider renting a gas-powered sod cutter. This powerful machine slices through sod like a hot knife through butter. It's important to dig down past the initial layer of topsoil or backfill until you reach subsoil. In most cases, digging down 8 to 10 inches is sufficient.

3 Fill the trench with gravel to within 4 inches of the top. Rent a gas-powered plate compactor and thoroughly tamp the gravel to create a solid, stable base. Spread 2 inches of stone dust on top of the gravel. Rake the surface smooth, then pound it flat with the compactor. Add a little more stone dust and sprinkle the surface with water, then compact the area once more. The water will mix with the dust, creating a cementlike bond.

Creating the border The first step in making the path's border is to install a temporary wooden form made from 1-by-3 boards. The 1 by 3s define the path's edges and support the soldier course of vertical bricks.

If the path is straight, hold a 1 by 3 on edge against each 1-by-2 stake; be sure the 1 by 3s are on the inside of the stakes. Tap each board down flush with the top of the grass. If necessary, use the claw of a hammer to scratch out a narrow trench beside the path. Fasten the 1 by 3s to the stakes with 1⅝-inch galvanized decking screws. (Drive the screws through the outside of the stake and into the form board where you can to make the job of removing the stakes and forms much easier.)

4 To follow any curves in the path, kerf the 1 by 3s so they'll bend. (Soak kerfed boards in water for an hour or so and they'll become supple and less likely to crack when you bend them.) Kerfing involves cross-cutting partway through the board, on the inside of the curve, creating slots (kerfs) that allow the board to bend. You can cut kerfs with a portable circular saw, but a radial-arm saw or slide-compound power miter saw is faster and safer. The kerfs should be ½ inch deep and about ⅜ inch apart for gentle curves.

In the same way as described above, install a 1-by-3 form along the opposite edge of the pathway, but this time set the boards ½ inch higher. This slight incline permits water to drain off the path's surface. Also measure between the two form boards in several places to be sure they're within ¼ inch of being perfectly parallel.

5 Along the inside of the 1-by-3 form boards, dig a 4-inch-wide trench about 7½ inches below the upper edge of the forms. Stand the first brick on end and use a rubber mallet to tap it down flush with the top of the form. Butt the next brick tightly against the first one. Tap it flush with the form board. Repeat for the remaining soldier bricks. Stop occasionally and lay a level across the 1-by-3 form boards to confirm that you're maintaining the ½-inch slope.

6 Rough-grade the stone dust over the gravel bed with a 2 by 4 (as shown), then final-grade by screeding to a uniform 2 inches below the top of the soldier-course bricks. Make a screed from a 2 by 4 that's 4 to 6 inches longer than the width of the pathway. Make a notch in each end that extends up from the bottom edge the thickness of the bricks less ⅛ inch. Then cut in equal amounts from the ends so that the uncut length of 2 by 4 between the notches measures ½ inch less than the width of the pathway between the perimeter soldier bricks. Place the screed with the "ears" riding on the soldier bricks (see top left of photo 7), and pull it toward you to rake the gravel to the correct height.

Setting the bricks The bricks are laid in two stages: first, the soldier course of vertical bricks is set along each edge of the pathway to create a solid border, and then the pathway bricks are laid in a basket-weave pattern to fill in.

tip: basket-weave pattern To create a basket-weave pattern, you must use bricks that are twice as long as they are wide. That's the only way to end up with consistent, perfectly aligned joints between the bricks.

Creating the border The first step in making the path's border is to install a temporary wooden form made from 1-by-3 boards. The 1 by 3s define the path's edges and support the soldier course of vertical bricks.

If the path is straight, hold a 1 by 3 on edge against each 1-by-2 stake; be sure the 1 by 3s are on the inside

8 Once all the bricks are set, spread a ½-inch layer of stone dust across the surface. Then, using a push broom with stiff bristles, sweep the stone dust back and forth across the pathway until all the brick joints are packed with dust.

9 Next, give the pathway a good soaking with a garden hose. The water will force the stone dust deep between the bricks. If necessary, sweep more stone dust across the bricks and wet the surface a second time. Finally, wait at least one week before removing the 1-by-2 stakes and 1-by-3 form boards.

CUTTING BRICKS TO FIT

Building a path with sharp curves or angles requires cutting some of the bricks. If you have only a few bricks to cut, use a mason's hammer to slowly chip the bricks down to size. Another option is to buy a wide mason's chisel, called a brick set, to chop the bricks in half. (Place the brick on the stone-dust surface before striking it with the brick set.) Both of these methods will work, but neither is very precise.

The easiest, most accurate way to cut brick is with a wet saw. This machine has a diamond-impregnated saw blade and a water pump that continuously bathes the spinning blade with cool water. The result is a perfectly smooth, precise cut. If you have a lot of cutting to do, it pays to rent a wet saw. To minimize rental fees, typically $40 to $60 a day, save all the cuts until the very end of the job. That way, you'll need the saw for the least amount of time.

flagstone path

A front walkway doesn't just lead to the front door. It should be an enhancement to the house, be comfortable and safe underfoot, and require very little maintenance. For an attractive and lasting first impression, consider flagstone. Because the joints are filled with rock rather than mortar, frost heaving won't crack the path, and any flagstones pushed out of place by freezing weather can be easily repositioned on the sand bedding. Preparing the walkway base and setting the stones involve some heavy labor, but once the work is complete, the walk will last for decades.

materials and tools

- flagstone (a local variety of your choice)
- sand or stone dust
- base or drain rock (1- to 2-inch diameter)
- crushed rock or ⅜-inch river rock for filling joints
- long hose or rope to mark out path
- landscaper's spray paint
- square-nose shovel
- level
- rubber mallet
- steel rake
- hammer
- brick set (mason's chisel)
- mattock and wheelbarrow, as needed
- gas-powered plate compactor or hand tamper
- safety glasses

1 Mark the proposed path outline by laying out a hose or rope. If you have an existing concrete walkway, you can remove it after first breaking it into manageable pieces with a rented jackhammer. Move the hoses around and look at the path from different angles until you feel satisfied. If possible, make the path about 4 feet wide, so two people can walk comfortably side by side. For a smooth transition at the house entryway and at the driveway, flare both ends of the walk. When you're satisfied, use landscaper's spray paint to mark the outline.

2 Although the flagstone itself will be bedded in sand, the entire walkway needs a solid foundation. Within the walkway outlines, dig down 8 inches to remove all soil or large rocks. Fill the excavated area with 5 inches of large-diameter unwashed drain rock. With a steel rake, level the gravel and then hand tamp (above), or use a rented gas-powered plate compactor, to thoroughly pack the base.

3 For a short walkway, bagged sand available at home-supply centers is convenient, but for larger projects get a truckload from a sand and gravel supplier. Use a steel rake to spread the sand about 2 inches thick over the pathway, bringing it up to about 1 inch below the adjoining grade. (For more convenient mowing, the finished walkway should be level with adjacent lawn.) The sand will allow you to more easily level the flagstone, which varies significantly in thickness.

4 If possible, start by laying out the flagstone pieces parallel to the sand-covered walkway. While adjusting the pattern, move the stones about on grass; making adjustments on the sand messes up the sand bed. Position the straightest edges along the pathway edges and beside the house entrance. Where necessary, shape the pieces with a hammer and brick set. Lay the flagstones out in a random pattern and fill in the spaces between the larger slabs with smaller pieces. A close fit is not necessary.

5 The final step is to fill the joints with crushed rock or $\frac{3}{8}$-inch river rock, both of which complement the flagstone and will not wash away, as sand can. Sweep the rock back and forth over the surface until all the spaces are filled. Once everything is in place, water the entire walkway thoroughly to further compact the rock between the joints.

mortared patio

There is a timeless elegance to a classic patio with the surface mortared in place, such as one made with bluestone, flagstone, or brick. Such patios will last years with little or no maintenance, as their materials generally become more attractive with age. However, a mortared patio requires a concrete slab for support. Without the slab, the bricks or stone will shift and the mortar will crack.

This project uses bluestone, which is a form of sandstone that looks like slate but is softer and less brittle. Bluestone is also easier to cut and fit than slate or flagstone. Ironically, bluestone is often not blue at all; colors include green, brown, bluish yellow, blue gray, and bluish purple. Bluestone may be sold in the form of rectangles 1 to $1\frac{1}{2}$ inches thick or in large irregular shapes similar to flagstone.

For small projects, you can generally pick out the pieces you want at the stone supplier. For larger projects, the stones will be delivered standing on edge in pallets. You select and lay them out from there.

tip: estimating concrete and gravel amounts

Concrete is ordered by the cubic yard. Gravel can be ordered by the cubic yard or by the ton; the supplier can readily convert the two. To determine how much you need, follow this formula: length × width × depth (all in feet) divided by 27 = cubic yards needed. As an example, consider a concrete slab that will be 18 feet long by 12 feet 6 inches wide and 4 inches thick. (Hint: 4 inches is $\frac{1}{3}$ foot.) That's 18 × 12.5 × .333 = 75 divided by 27, or 2.77 cubic yards of concrete needed. Add 5–10 percent to all orders so you don't run short.

Lay out the site For a patio that will be built adjoining a residence, drive two short 2-by-4 stakes firmly into the ground next to the house to mark each side of the patio. Into the face of each stake, drive a drywall screw about 18 inches above the planned height of the slab. (If you can put a screw into the house siding, do that instead of using stakes.) Use a water level or laser level to ensure the screws are at the same height. Tie mason's string to the screws and then, following the line from a framing square held against the house, pull the string out from the house at a 90-degree angle past the end of the slab area. The 90-degree angle is only approximate at this point and will be made exact after batter boards are built.

Construct batter boards You'll need several sets of batter boards to precisely position string that defines the sides and ends of the slab. Each set of batter boards consists of two sharpened 2-by-4 stakes with a 1-by-4 crosspiece attached. In line with string from the house that marks the two sides of the patio, position the batter boards about 3 feet beyond the end of the patio so you have room to work without bumping them; if the batter boards move after they are built, the foundation lines will be thrown off. After driving the stakes firmly into the ground about 3 feet apart, use a transit, laser level, or water

level to set the tops of all crosspieces at 18 inches. Attach the crosspieces with drywall screws so you do not disturb the stakes. Place another set of batter boards to mark the end of the patio, as shown above.

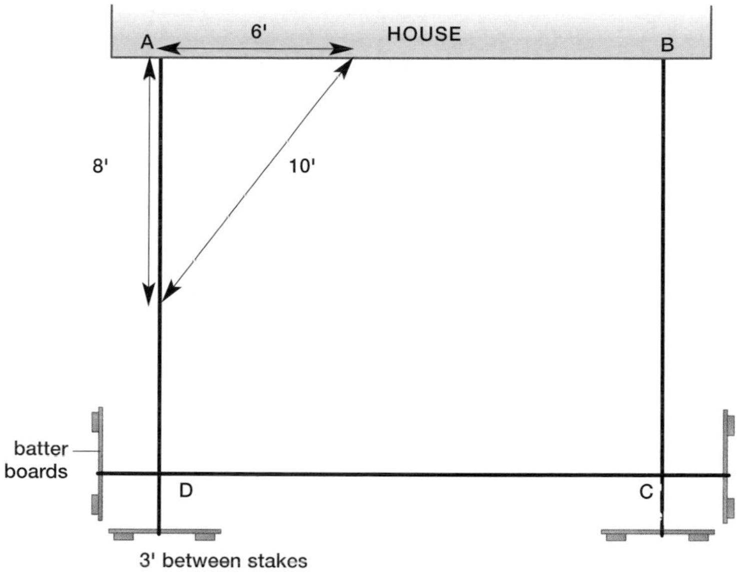

Establish right angles To establish an exact right angle from the house to the first set of batter boards, use the 3-4-5 method. The Pythagorean rule states that when the sides of a triangle are exactly 3, 4, and 5 feet long, the angle opposite the longest side will be a right angle. You can use multiples of 3-4-5, such as 6-8-10, for even greater accuracy. In this case, measure from point A on the house toward point B and mark at 6 feet. Now have a helper pull the string tight between A and D while you

mark the 8-foot point on the string with tape or a pen. Pull a tape measure from the 6-foot mark on the house toward the 8-foot mark on the string. Have a helper move the string back and forth until the 8-foot mark falls exactly under the 10-foot mark on your tape. This indicates an exact right angle. Mark where the string crosses the crosspiece of the batter board, drive a nail, and tie it off. Repeat the process between B and C, and then D and C. Double-check your work by measuring the diagonals between A and C and D and B. When the measurements are exactly the same, the outline is square. Use a pencil to mark where the lines cross the batter boards so you can readily remove and replace the string as needed.

ESTABLISHING A RIGHT ANGLE WITH THE 3-4-5 METHOD

- bluestone pavers
- mortar mix (to set pavers)
- Portland cement and sand (to mix for paver grout)
- crushed rock (for slab base)
- concrete
- 2-by-4 form boards
- ¼-by-4-inch hardboard or plywood for curving form boards (if needed)
- 2-by-4 stakes and 1-by-4 crosspieces (for batter boards)
- drywall screws
- 6-inch mesh reinforcing wire, or ½-inch (#4) rebar
- dobies (to support wire or rebar)
- 6-mil plastic sheeting
- water level, laser level, or transit
- large pieces of scrap plywood for kneeling boards
- digging tools, such as shovel, mattock, and rake
- vibrating plate compactor
- screed, to level wet concrete
- circular saw with diamond-tipped blade
- contractor's wheelbarrow
- tape measure
- 4-foot level
- mason's string
- chalk line
- control-joint trowel
- narrow tuck pointing trowel
- wide concrete trowel
- rubber mallet
- sponge and bucket
- grout bag
- hammer
- cordless drill
- framing square
- wax pencil
- ear and eye protection
- rubber boots and work gloves

ANATOMY OF A PAVED PATIO ON A SLAB FOUNDATION

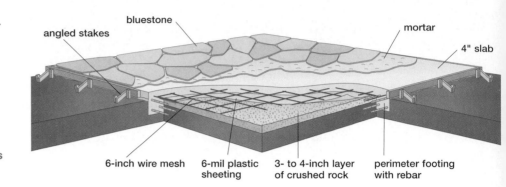

angled stakes — bluestone — mortar — 4" slab

6-inch wire mesh — 6-mil plastic sheeting — 3- to 4-inch layer of crushed rock — perimeter footing with rebar

1 Using the string lines as a guide, install 2-by-4 form boards around the perimeter. The inside face of the forms should be directly beneath the string line. Begin by establishing where the top of the forms will be against the house and snap a level chalk line there. By measuring down from the string lines to the tops of the form boards, establish a slope away from the house of 1 inch for every 8 feet. This will prevent water from pooling on the finished patio. Construct the forms by attaching the 2 by 4s to stakes with drywall screws through the stake into the board. Place a stake every 3 feet and behind all butted joints. (For curved sections, use ¼-inch-thick hardboard.) Position the bottom edge of the 2-by-4 form boards ½ inch above grade so the slab will be a full 4 inches thick (concrete won't leak out). Vertical stakes will support the forms, but for added support, fasten additional stakes driven at an angle to the forms (see illustration).

2

2 A concrete slab needs a base of packed gravel and a perimeter footing to prevent it from moving and cracking. Within the slab outline, remove all vegetation and soil 6 inches down. Then, just inside the perimeter, dig a trench 6 inches wide and at least 6 inches deeper than the excavation (or to the frostline) as the footing ditch (check local codes for needed footing depth). For the base material, use crushed rock, sometimes called road base. The material has rough, irregular edges that will lock together when compacted. To determine how much you need, calculate the number of cubic yards (see tip, page 94). When the crushed rock arrives, have friends lined up with wheelbarrows to transfer it to the slab site. Rake it level, keeping most of it out of the footing trench. Once the crushed rock is level, use a rented vibrating plate compactor to pack it firmly. If you live in an area with a high water table, cover the base with 6-mil plastic sheeting before putting down the reinforcement and the concrete. This will keep high water from percolating up through the concrete.

3

3 To strengthen the slab and minimize cracking, reinforce it with wire or iron bars. Welded reinforcing wire with 6-inch mesh comes in rolls 5 feet and 7 feet wide and varying lengths. To use it, unroll the length needed and flatten it on the ground before putting it on the rock base. All reinforcement, whether wire or rebar, must be supported off the ground so it is in the bottom third of the pour. If the reinforcement lies flat on the ground, it does no good. If using rebar, space the bars across

the length of the slab area in a 12-inch-wide pattern. Tie each intersection with wire. Once the reinforcement is in place, raise the frame off the ground by placing small concrete support blocks, called dobies, under every third or fourth cross-piece. Likewise, in the footing ditch, place two lengths of rebar on dobies along the bottom of the trench and hang others on wire from the form boards. Bend rebar around the corners, overlap all joined pieces by 14 inches, and wire them together.

4 Now you're ready for the concrete, and lots of friends to help. The concrete mixer truck will have a chute that adjusts up to 16 feet long for placing the concrete. If the truck cannot park near the pour, tell the concrete supplier you will need a concrete pumper, as was used in this project. Start placing the concrete in the section near the house and work toward the other end. As your helpers spread the concrete, have them work it a few times with a shovel to settle it and force out air bubbles.

4

more formal appearance by cutting the stones into random shapes.

Once the slab has cured for two or three days, you can begin laying the stone. Start by setting out about a dozen pieces on the slab. Mix smaller stones with the larger ones, looking for sides that roughly match another piece of stone.

6 Start by cutting a straight edge along pieces that will fit against the house foundation. Using a level as a straightedge, mark the line using a wax pencil, and then cut with a diamond-tipped saw blade in a circular saw. Bluestone cuts easily, but to significantly prolong the life of the blade, have a helper run a stream of water on the blade to lubricate it while you cut.

There are two ways to cut patterns. The first is to lay the edge of one stone close to another, draw a line on one that roughly matches the outline of the other, and then cut. For more precise work, place the edge of the cut piece on the other one, mark the outline, and cut, making sweeping curves and angles rather than many straight lines. Make one cut about ¼ inch deep as a guide, and then make a second, deeper pass. Depending on the stone, you generally need to cut only about three-quarters of the way through, then hit the waste side with a hammer to snap it off. Continue cutting and placing until the patio is covered with bluestone in the desired pattern. Joints should be between ½ and ¾ inch wide.

5 After 3 or 4 feet of concrete has been poured, begin screeding while others continue placing the concrete. A screed is a straight 2-by board on edge that is long enough to reach across the slab. With a person on each end, work the screed back and forth across the concrete to level it flush with the top of the forms. One person just ahead of the screed must shovel excess concrete out of the way and fill in low spots. Once a section is done, screed it once more and then move on.

Laying out the stone There is a bit of an art to laying out bluestone pieces—it's somewhat like assembling a jigsaw puzzle. It may seem confusing at first, but you will soon get a feeling for how the pieces are going to fit. For an informal look, the stones can be placed so they fit only approximately, with wide areas of grout filling in spaces. Create a

7 All the stones should be mortared in place just where you laid them out (see box below). Starting beside the house, tilt the first piece up and wet both the underside of the stone and the concrete slab with a sponge and water. This prevents the mortar from drying too fast. Set the stone to one side and smooth a 1-inch-thick layer of mortar in the space. Put the stone on the mortar and tap it with a rubber mallet. The stones should be set about half their thickness into the mortar. As you work, mortar will be pushed up between the joints. Using a narrow tuck pointing trowel, remove this mortar down to the base of the stone. Later, you will fill this space with grout.

8 Keeping the stones level with each other is essential as you progress. Start by mortaring the stones in place along each side. Then lay a long, straight 2 by 4 on edge across the patio and use it as a guide to keep the stones flush with each other as you work. You can also stretch string across the patio about 1 inch above the rocks, but it is easier to move a 2 by 4. Use a level on each stone as you set it to ensure that it is level side to side but still follows the slope of the patio slab. If a stone is too high, tap it down with a rubber mallet; if it is too low, lift it up and add more mortar.

9 Let the mortar set for 36 hours and then grout the joints. To make grout, mix one part Type II Portland cement and one part fine sand. Mix thoroughly, and to the consistency of toothpaste. For large spaces between stones, you can apply grout with a trowel. For narrow spaces, as in this case, a grout bag, which is similar to a cake-decorating bag, is ideal. Fill the bag with grout and then squeeze the mix into each joint, filling it completely. As soon as you empty the bag, smooth the joints with the back of a trowel. The grout should be flat and flush with the surface, not concave, which will trap water and ice. When you've finished, sprinkle the entire patio with water and then cover it with plastic sheeting for 72 hours while the grout cures. Keep the patio damp at all times during this period.

Spills of grout are inevitable. Scrape up excess with your trowel. Then, three days later when the grout is set, wash the stones with a heavy sponge and water to remove the thin layer of grout that remains where spills occurred.

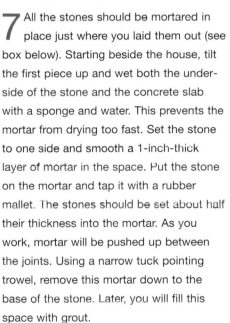

tip: mixing mortar You can buy ready-mix mortar, but you will save money by mixing your own, particularly for a large patio. To make your own, use Type II Portland cement, which contains lime to make the mix more pliable. Mix one part cement to three parts sand, and then add water slowly until the mortar is the consistency of toothpaste. The mortar should "stand up" when placed, not run out flat. Mix the mortar in a wheelbarrow with a square-tipped shovel or hoe, or in a rented concrete mixer for larger jobs. Make sure it's well mixed, and prepare only what you can use in about 30 minutes.

garden steps

On sloping ground, garden steps become an inviting pathway to a new vista. On a more practical level, steps make it easier to get around on a hilly yard. Pressure-treated 4-by-6 timbers, available at home centers, make good do-it-yourself garden steps (see page 34 for more on pressure-treated wood).

Like steps around a deck or house, garden steps should be consistent in riser height and tread depth. Where the terrain slopes gradually, you may want each step separated by several feet of walkway. Steep slopes, however, require a flight of steps. Where the

materials and tools

- **4 by 6s, one 8-foot length for each step, pressure treated for ground contact (.40 pounds preservative retention per cubic foot)**
- **2-foot lengths of ½-inch (#4) rebar, two for each step**
- **crushed rock**
- **sand**
- **landscape fabric**
- **copper naphthenate preservative to treat cut ends and drilled holes**
- **tape measure**
- **long, straight 2 by 4 or pole**
- **level**
- **square-nose shovel and mattock**
- **hacksaw, if needed to cut rebar**
- **drill with ⅜-inch by 14-inch-long bit**
- **circular saw**
- **hand tamper**
- **dust mask, goggles, and gloves for working with preserved wood**

grade changes from a gradual slope to a steep one, you may decide on a combination approach, with a landing or other clear transition that separates the two areas.

The best height for risers is 7+ inches, with an accompanying tread that is 10+ inches deep; shorter risers are fine, however, as long as the tread depth is increased. (Using the timbers shown here, the riser height is about 4 inches, which calls for a tread depth of about 13 inches.) And because it's more comfortable to navigate wide stairs, make steps at

least 4 feet wide where possible. This allows two or more people to easily walk or sit side by side. For 4-foot-wide steps, cut two 2-foot sides and one 4-foot front riser from each 8-foot timber.

Because a standard circular saw will not cut through a 4 by 6 in one pass, use a square to mark the cut line completely around the timber, then cut it with a pass on each side (treat the cut ends with copper naphthenate). The long piece will form the first riser, and the two short pieces will support subsequent risers.

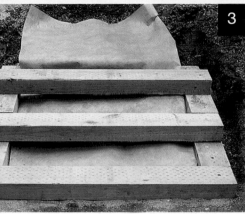

1 Starting at the bottom of the slope, roughly level the ground for the first step. Use a square-tipped shovel and a mattock to remove about 2 inches of soil beneath where the timbers will be placed, and then fill with sand. (It is much easier to level the timber by adding or removing sand than it is to level the ground.) Set the timber with the 4-by dimension as the riser. Use a level to ensure that the timber is level from side to side and back to front.

Extend the support pieces into the hillside from each end of the long timber. Again, excavate deeper than needed and add sand to level these pieces. Ensure that the end of each support piece fits snugly and smoothly against the long riser.

2 To keep the step from moving, drill a ⅜-inch-diameter hole through each end of the timber, treat the hole with copper naphthenate, and then drive a 2-foot length of ½-inch rebar through it into the ground. Repeat this process with each side support piece. For each successive step, drill through both the step and the support pieces and fasten them together with the lengths of rebar.

3 Place the next riser on top of the side pieces. Position it in from the leading edge of the first riser by the depth of the tread, 13 inches in this case. Dig into the slope just enough to place the side support pieces for the second step, again ensuring they are level. Remove enough soil in the middle to fit the riser in place. Continue up the slope in this manner. When all the steps are in place, but before filling in behind the risers, spread landscape cloth over the exposed earth to prevent weeds. Finally, fill the tread areas with crushed rock and pack with a hand tamper.

To determine the number of steps needed on a slope, measure the length of the slope and the total rise. To measure the rise, extend a long 2 by 4 or pole out from the top of the slope, check that it is level, and measure down on a plumb line to the bottom of the slope. (For long slopes, do this in stages and then total the measurements.)

Convert total rise to inches and divide that number by the riser height (in this case, the thickness of the timbers being used for the steps). The result is the number of risers that will be required. To find the tread depth, divide the length of the slope by the number of risers.

Example: In this project, the slope is 12 inches high and 39 inches long. The step material is about 4 inches thick. To find the number of steps, divide the total rise of 12 inches by 4 (the riser height), which indicates there will be 3 steps. (Round up if the result isn't even.) Then divide the length of the slope (in inches) by the number of steps. In this case, that's 39 inches divided by 3 steps, indicating the proper tread depth is 13 inches.

basic deck

A deck, like a patio, is really an outside room that can be used for entertaining friends or just relaxing on your own. Decks can be any shape imaginable, from the basic square to elaborately curved and shaped structures. They can be attached to the house, as in this example, or be free-standing around a garden pond, in a grove of trees, or winding beside a flower garden. Where you must deal with steep or difficult terrain, a multi-level deck can provide the solution.

Although heart cedar and redwood are still widely used for decking in the West, alternative materials have made significant gains in recent years across the country. Synthetic decking, which includes vinyl, plastic, and composite wood, continues to gain popularity because it is easy to maintain. Certain tropical hardwoods, such as ipé and meranti, make excellent, although expensive decking materials. Despite being the least attractive alternative, pressure-treated wood is used just about universally for deck support structures—and often for decking itself—because of its durability, strength, and low cost.

DECK PLAN OVERVIEW

house

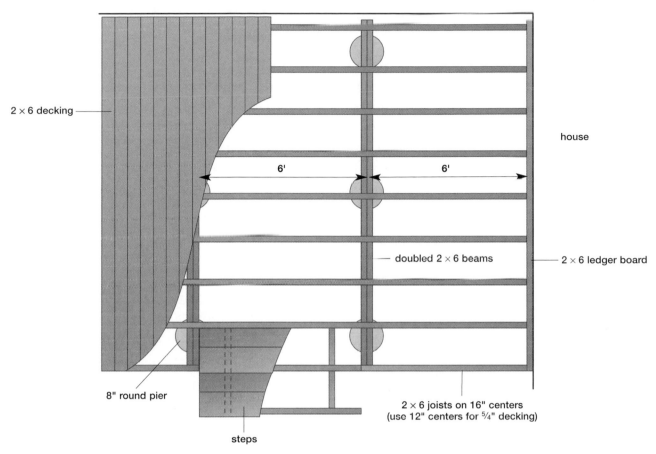

2 × 6 decking

house

6'   6'

doubled 2 × 6 beams

2 × 6 ledger board

8" round pier

steps

2 × 6 joists on 16" centers
(use 12" centers for ⁵/₄" decking)

Some people prefer to leave their wood decks untreated, letting them go gray naturally. Others try to maintain the color of new wood, but this is a losing battle, even if you refinish it every year. Ultraviolet light and water penetration are the main problems. Penetrating, clear finishes that include anti-fungal preservatives and water resistors, help and can be used to keep some of the natural look. But they must be renewed more often and provide no UV protection, which is where stains come in. Transparent stains offer a little UV protection, semi-transparent stains much more.

FOOTING DETAIL

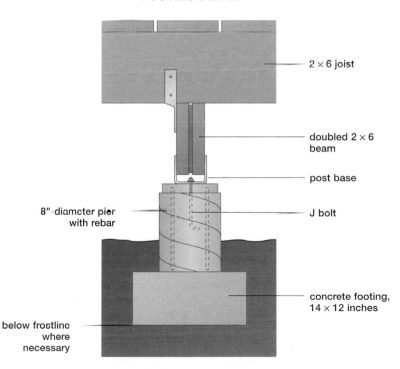

2 × 6 joist

doubled 2 × 6
beam

post base

8"-diameter pier
with rebar

J bolt

concrete footing,
14 × 12 inches

below frostline
where
necessary

Installing the ledger board

Decks that are attached to a house are connected with a pressure-treated ledger board. Attached improperly, the deck could collapse or, almost as bad, water could become trapped between the ledger and the house, causing rot. Ledger boards are either bolted to rim joists, screwed into wall studs or the sill plate, or bolted to masonry with ½-inch expansion bolts.

First locate the top of the ledger board so the decking surface will be just 1 to 2 inches below the door threshold; this will prevent people from tripping. If the decking must be much lower, position it 4 to 8 inches down so it is clearly a step.

The best way to attach a ledger board is with bolts through a rim joist, because the nut on the other side of the bolt provides security. Use one ½-inch-diameter bolt every 16 inches and be sure the bolts do not line up with where the deck joists will go.

If the rim joist is not accessible, then connect the ledger board by fastening lag screws into studs or the sill plate. This is more challenging because you need to line up the bolt with the center of the 2-by lumber. If you use this method, use ½-inch-diameter lag screws that are 6 inches long in each stud, and make sure the screw is securely fastened into solid wood. Just to make sure all is strong and safe, Tom Silva uses both thru bolts and lag screws, as shown below.

If the siding surface is irregular, typical of vinyl, aluminum, shingles, and wood siding, you will need to cut off a section and install flashing between the ledger and the house. Use a circular saw with a carborundum blade, set slightly deeper than the siding thickness, and cut out an area 1 inch larger than the ledger all around. Cover this opening with self-adhering waterproofing membrane, positioning the upper edge under the siding and the lower part over the bare area and an inch or so below. Attach the ledger to the rim joist with bolts, or to studs (or sill plate) with lag screws every 16 inches. Space the ledger away from the house at least ½ inch with rot-resistant wood spacers, or use four galvanized washers on the bolt or screw between the ledger board and siding. Spacing the ledger out in this manner will allow water to run past without being trapped, which is the surest way to prevent rot.

Then position a strip of self-adhering waterproofing membrane up under the siding on top and down over the ledger board, topping that with a strip of aluminum or copper flashing, also under the siding and bent to fit over the ledger board. To finish, seal the flashing edges with polyurethane caulk. For a house with smooth siding, such as plywood or stucco, you don't need to use flashing over the ledger board. Instead, use caulk liberally around all lag screw and bolt holes and space the ledger away from the house as described above.

Laying out the site To establish the deck outline and ensure that it is square, erect batter boards as described on page 95. Use a water level, laser level, or builder's level to set all the tops of the crosspieces the exact same height as the top of the ledger. Note that string lines are pulled from two directions to exactly position the deck perimeter, the corners, and the footing holes.

ATTACHING THE DECK TO THE HOUSE

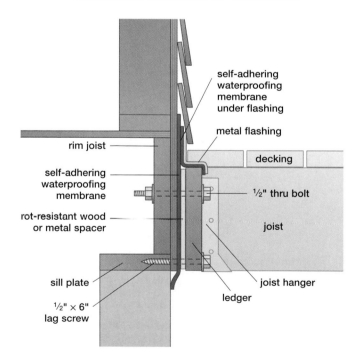

- rim joist
- self-adhering waterproofing membrane
- rot-resistant wood or metal spacer
- sill plate
- ½" × 6" lag screw
- self-adhering waterproofing membrane under flashing
- metal flashing
- decking
- ½" thru bolt
- joist
- joist hanger
- ledger

- lumber for beams, posts, and decking
- 8-inch-diameter cardboard tube forms and ready-mix concrete
- ½-inch (#4) rebar (for footings)
- self-adhering waterproofing membrane (if needed)
- aluminum or copper flashing
- ½-inch hot-dipped galvanized lag screws, bolts, or expansion bolts to fasten ledger
- face-mounted joist hangers and nails
- 12d and 16d hot-dipped galvanized nails
- J-bolts
- Post bases

- deck board fasteners, vinyl-coated screws, or waterproof marine glue
- posthole digger and shovel
- hammer
- level—water, laser, or builder's
- ½-inch drill and ⅜- and ½-inch bits
- mason's string
- handsaw and circular saw
- contractor's wheelbarrow
- plumb bob
- framing and combination squares
- stair gauges
- tape measure and calculator
- gloves, dust mask, and eye protection (essential if using pressure-treated wood)

1 To determine the exact center of the six concrete support columns for this deck, drop a plumb bob where the string lines cross and mark each spot with a small stake. Remove the string lines and dig the footing holes. In areas where the ground does not freeze, make the holes a minimum of 14 inches in diameter and 12 inches deep. In colder climates, the footing must be below the frostline.

2 Fill the footing hole to within 2 inches of grade with ready-mix concrete, and then push two lengths of rebar down into the concrete. Then push the 8-inch card-board tube form down into the wet con-crete slightly. (Some areas permit the use of hardened vinyl footing forms that attach to the tubes; check with your local building inspector's office.) Pull the string line tem-porarily along the side of the tube form and mark with a pencil. Remember, this marks the top of the ledger, so deduct the exact depth of the joists and the beams and cut the tube at that height with a handsaw. Fill the tube form with concrete and recheck plumb. Repeat for each column.

3 As each row of tube forms is filled, pull the string lines again and use a plumb bob to mark the center of the concrete-filled tubes. Set a J-bolt directly in each center to later accept the post base (see page 103). Allow the concrete to cure overnight.

4 The traditional way to space beams is to check span tables. They tell you how much distance a beam or joist can span, which depends upon its size and the type of wood. This deck was designed using built-up beams of Douglas fir made by nailing two 2 by 6s together, a technique that Tom Silva uses to simplify deck building. Tom has a rule of thumb for this method: the beam's nominal width in inches should match the span in feet. For example, a 10-foot span requires two 2 by 10s. For the 6-foot span between the two piers in this deck, the beams were formed by two 2 by 6s nailed together.

Before forming the beam, sight down the top edge of each board to make sure

the crown, or edge curve in the board, is facing up. Nail the boards together with 12d galvanized nails placed in a zigzag pattern every 16 inches. Before nailing the 2 by 6s together, place narrow strips of ½" exterior plywood between them. The spacers allow water and air circulation around the beam, and also allow the beam to fit snugly in the post base. Anchor the beam in place with 12d nails through the post base.

5 Joists are normally the same size as the ledger board. For a deck that has just one side attached to the house and is open on the other three sides, first nail the two outside joists to the ends of the ledger board. Then adjust them on the beams until they are equidistant from each other and the diagonal measurements are equal, indicating the layout is square. Then install the joist hangers on the ledger in between.

Where the deck fits against an L-shaped house, as here, install the inside joist approximately 3 inches out from the wall. Place one end in a joist hanger on the ledger and check that the joist is equally spaced from the house for its full length. Toenail the joist where it crosses each beam. Nail the outside joist to the end of the ledger board and then adjust it until the diagonal measurements are equal.

To locate the joist hangers between the inner and outer joist, begin measuring from the center of the inside joist and mark every 16 inches on the top of the ledger board.

When positioning the joist hangers on the ledger, use a short length of joist material in the hanger so the top is flush with the top of the ledger, as shown above. Center the material on the mark and attach the joist hangers with joist hanger nails.

6 Next, put the joists, crown side up, in the joist hangers and toenail them to the beams with 16d nails. Fasten the joists to the hangers with joist hanger nails. To perfectly align the joist ends, wait until all joists are installed, snap a chalk line where you want them to end, and cut.

7 When installing decking, let the
boards run long and trim them all
later. If the deck is longer than a single
board can reach, stagger the joints so
there is no visible pattern. Select the
straightest board for the first row beside
the house.

Fasten the deck boards over each joist.
The least effective and least attractive way
is to simply nail the boards on. Vinyl-coated
screws, colored to match the type of
decking, are fast to install and have great
holding power. Alternatively, choose from
a variety of hidden deck fasteners, one of
which is shown here. All come with detailed
installation instructions. You can also use
Tom Silva's method: put waterproof marine
glue over each joist and add a few ran-
domly spaced stainless-steel finish nails
to hold them down until the glue sets.

8 Decking generally needs to be spaced
the width of an 8d nail to allow rainwater to drain and to allow for expansion.
Driving the nail through a scrap piece of
plywood keeps it from falling through the
crack (as shown at right). If using very wet
lumber, however, position the boards so
they are just touching. As they dry, they
will shrink to the proper spacing.

Deck boards are often warped and
must be straightened during installation.
To do this, fasten one end of the board
in the proper position and then push the
bowed area into line and fasten it. For
stubborn boards, or when you need to
move one an inch or less, pry the board
into place with a chisel. First, anchor the
chisel by driving the tip into the joist
beside the bowed board, as shown. Then
push the handle forward to move the
board. Fasten the board into place while
holding it in line.

Building steps Whether you are building stairs within your house or steps against your deck, the principles remain the same. The most difficult part of building steps is determining the riser height and tread depth. After that, it's basic carpentry. Before you begin, it helps to understand the terminology:

- Riser: height of each step
- Tread: depth of each step
- Run: how far out the stairs extend
- Stringer: notched supports beneath the stairs, usually cut from 2-by-12 pressure-treated wood

ATTACHING STEPS TO A DECK

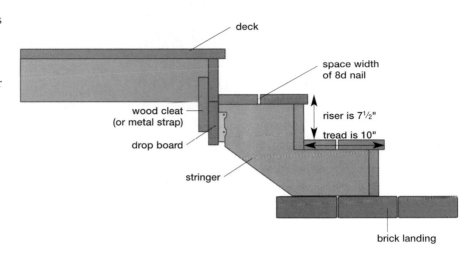

deck

space width of 8d nail

wood cleat (or metal strap)

riser is 7½"

tread is 10"

drop board

stringer

brick landing

STAIR CALCULATIONS

Here's how to determine how many steps will be needed and the riser height of each step:

1. Measure the distance in inches from the deck's finished surface to the ground. This is the total rise.

2. Divide the total rise by 8, which is an average stair riser height, and round the answer off to the nearest whole number. That is the number of risers (or steps) you'll need.

3. Determine the actual height of each riser by dividing the total rise by the number of steps. Round off to the nearest ¾ inch for the exact riser height.

Example: The distance from the deck to the ground for the deck shown on these pages is 22¾ inches, or 22.75 inches. Divide by 8 to get 2.84, or, rounded off to the nearest whole

number, 3 risers total. To find the exact riser height, divide the total rise by 3. The answer—7.58, or 7½ inches (rounded to the nearest ¼ inch)—is the height of each riser. Note that this method puts the top step on the same level as the deck. To make the first step one riser down (as shown above), lay out one step less on your stair stringers so they rest on the edge of the deck (a drop board, as shown in step 11, may be necessary).

4. To find the tread depth, remember this formula: riser height plus tread depth should equal 17 to 17½ inches. So to find the tread depth, subtract the riser height from 17½ inches, in this case 10 inches.

5. To find the total run, multiply the tread depth times the number of stairs, in this case 10 × 2 = 20 inches. Knowing the total run enables you to build the landing in advance.

9 Use a framing square to lay out tread and riser cuts on the 2-by-12 stringers. Following the example on page 109, put the narrower leg of the square (called the tongue) on the 7½-inch mark and the wider leg (the blade) on the 10-inch mark, as shown. Stair gauges that clamp to the square will maintain the correct measurements as you move the square. Alternatively, use Tom Silva's trick of clamping a straightedge to the framing square at the desired tread and riser heights.

Mark off the first step and then move the level down the stringer until aligned with the previous mark. Lay out the next step. Continue like this for all the steps. To make the plumb cut on the stringer, go back to the top and carry the first riser line all the way across the 2 by 12.

Finally, and importantly, shorten the stringer at the bottom by the thickness of the tread, which in this case is 1½ inches. This allows for the fact that there is no tread thickness to account for on the ground.

10 Cut the stair stringer with a circular saw according to your pattern. In this example, the material to be removed is marked with an X. Use a handsaw to finish off the cut at each juncture between the tread and the riser.

12 Once the stringers are in place, install the treads and risers, starting with the risers. The risers should fit so that no space is visible at the top or bottom when the tread is in place. If necessary, rip wider boards to fit and then install them. Outdoor stair treads are often made of two 2-by boards with a $\frac{1}{8}$-inch space between them for rainwater to drain through. The front of the tread should overhang the riser below by 1 inch or so. You may need to mix 2 by 4s, 2 by 6s, or 2 by 8s to get the exact fit, or rip the inside board narrower.

11 Put the stringer in place to check for fit. When satisfied, use that stringer as a pattern to mark the remaining stringers. For stairs more than 3 feet wide, use a center stringer for additional support. Make sure the stringers are equally spaced and then attach them to the joist hangers with joist hanger nails. (You'll have to notch the top of the stringer on the underside to make the joist hangers fit.)

If you want the first tread to be one step lower than the deck, the rim joist may not extend low enough to hang the stringers. In this case, make a drop board, also called a hanger board. Make one by nailing 1-by-4 cleats or metal fasteners to the back of the drop board, fitting it edge to edge with the bottom of the joist, and then attach it.

retaining wall

A wide variety of landscaping projects can enhance the look—and value—of your house. Some beautify with lush plantings and flowering trees. Others help solve a specific problem, such as laying a drainage pipe (see page 70) to carry away runoff. A retaining wall is one of the few landscaping features that can both improve the appearance of your property and remedy a problem area.

Retaining walls can tame hilly terrain and turn steeply pitched slopes into relatively flat, usable land. And if you choose an appropriate building material, the wall will not only perform its duty but become a dramatic landscape feature. Case in point: the attractive retaining wall shown here, which borders and holds back the slope around a narrow driveway to a house that sits atop a knoll.

The wall, which replaced one of rotting timber, is constructed of interlocking precast concrete blocks that look like old cobblestones. The blocks are dry-stacked, meaning they have no mortar between them. Instead, each block has a recessed groove molded into its bottom surface and a raised ridge running along its top. As the courses are laid, the ridges fit into the grooves, effectively locking the blocks together. The advantages of this type of wall, which is known as a segmental wall, are that it goes up very quickly and costs significantly less than a traditional mortared field-stone wall. Also, unlike a wall built of wooden landscaping timbers, it will last virtually forever.

ANATOMY OF A RETAINING WALL

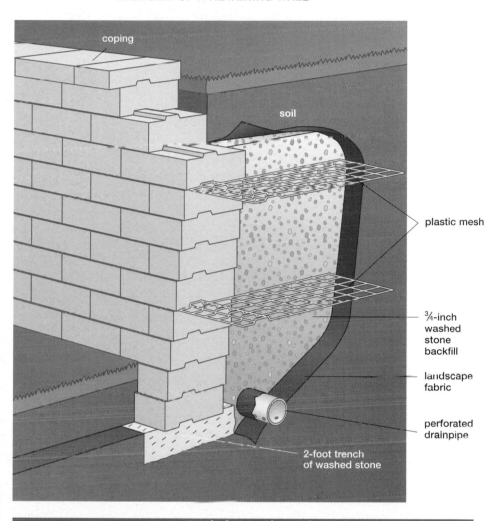

coping

soil

plastic mesh

¾-inch washed stone backfill

landscape fabric

perforated drainpipe

2-foot trench of washed stone

materials and tools

- interlocking precast concrete blocks and coping stones
- ¾-inch washed round stone
- stone dust
- landscape fabric
- plastic reinforcement mesh (geogrid)
- 4-inch-diameter perforated PVC pipe
- masonry adhesive caulk

- spray paint
- level
- string
- gas-powered plate compactor
- block splitter or masonry wet saw
- skid-steer loader (optional)
- backhoe (optional)
- rubber mallet
- ear and eye protection

Excavating the site The weight of wet soil leaning against a wall can topple even the sturdiest structure. Therefore, the first step is to remove some soil from the hillside to make room for perforated drainage pipe and crushed-stone backfill.

The amount of soil to excavate depends on the site specifics, including soil type and wall height. But a good rule of thumb is 1 foot of hillside for each foot of wall height. So, for a 3-foot-tall wall, you will need to dig back 3 feet. Walls taller than 4 feet need to be engineered and typically require tiebacks for added stability (see tip on opposite page).

1 Start by outlining the perimeter of the proposed wall on the ground with spray paint. (In this case, the wall was outlined beyond the old lawn, farther up on the hill.) Then, hire a backhoe operator to tear out the old retaining wall, if necessary, and to remove the appropriate amount of soil from the hillside.

2 To ensure that the wall is stable, begin by digging a 2-foot-wide trench, at least 2 feet deep, along the wall's outline. (In cold-weather regions, you must dig the trench down to the frostline to prevent frost heave from damaging the wall.) Fill the trench to within 2 inches of the top with ³⁄₄-inch washed stone. Rake the surface smooth, then tamp the stone flat with a gas-powered plate compactor. Top the compacted stone base with 2 inches of stone dust. Lightly sprinkle the surface with water and tamp it flat.

Setting the first course The first course of blocks forms the foundation for the wall, meaning it must be perfectly level. If not, it won't support the subsequent courses and the wall will fail. Or the wall will develop "ripples" and not look right.

3 Set a string at the right height for the first course and lay the first block in place with the ridged edge facing up. Level the block in two directions, tapping it with a rubber mallet if necessary. Continue setting blocks in the first course, butting them tightly and leveling each one. Once the course is complete, check all the blocks once again for level. Errors in this first row will be magnified as the wall rises.

Drainage Spread landscape fabric over the entire excavated area, starting from the base of the wall and running up the slope. Be sure to leave enough material to fold back later over the top of the completed wall. This water-permeable fabric prevents the retained soil from clogging the drainage stone and drainpipe.

Wrap a length of 4-inch-diameter perforated PVC pipe in landscape fabric and lay it (holes facing down) along the back of the first course of blocks. It will drain away water that collects at the base of the wall. Be sure the pipe angles down toward the low end of the wall, about 1 inch for every 4 feet of length. Then cover the fabric-wrapped pipe with a 6-inch layer of ¾-inch washed stone. Tamp the stone flat with the plate compactor.

Laying blocks With the first course completed, the rest of the wall goes up rather quickly, thanks to the blocks' ridge-and-groove system, which not only aligns the units but also automatically steps back each subsequent course by ¾ inch. The primary concern in stacking this type of block is to make sure that you stagger the vertical seams for a more natural look.

To avoid settling behind the wall, backfill behind each course with the washed stone. Rake the stone smooth and compact it flat. After every

fourth course, lay down a sheet of plastic reinforcement mesh (geogrid), which ties the wall and backfill into a single, immovable mass. Lay the front edge of the mesh over the ridges running along the tops of the blocks. That way, it will be securely held in place when the next course of blocks is laid on top. Continue setting blocks in this manner until you reach the top of the wall.

4 Once the last course is set, the wall is ready for the system's coping stones, which are grooved on the bottom but smooth on top. Apply a thick bead of masonry adhesive caulk to the blocks along the top of the wall, then set the coping stones in place. Continue to install coping stones along the entire length of the wall. Next, fold the landscape fabric over the stone backfill and trim it just below the second-to-the-last course. Cover the fabric with a foot of amended soil, then plant grass or shrubs.

tip: watch that height For retaining walls taller than 4 feet, check with your supplier for engineering specifics; or hire an architect or civil engineer to examine the site and draw plans.

mortared stone wall

For centuries, stone walls have been used to define boundaries, corral livestock, and separate gardens from pastures. Today, stone walls are still popular, though they are more commonly built alongside driveways, swimming pools, flowerbeds, and patios.

To build a stone wall, you need more than a pile of rocks and a strong back. Careful planning is required, as well as the skilled eye of a treasure hunter in order to find the perfect stone to fit each spot on the wall. Carefully crafted, a stone wall will last for generations.

If you've considered building a stone wall on your property, the low, double-faced patio wall shown here is a fairly simple project. This wall is built of a relatively hard fieldstone, which is mostly soft granite, and mortared, meaning that each stone is set in a fresh bed of mortar. Mortaring creates a wall that's much stronger and more durable—and easier to build—than a dry-stacked wall.

For quantities of fieldstone, crushed stone, mortar, rebar, and concrete, check with your materials supplier.

- select-grade fieldstone
- crushed stone
- concrete
- ½-inch-diameter rebar (#4), 3 times the wall length
- mortar mix
- gas-powered plate compactor
- ¼-inch hardboard or plywood
- saw for ripping boards (table, circular, or radial-arm)
- 3-foot-long wooden stakes (2 by 2s, 1 by 3s, or 1 by 4s) for stringline
- metal or wood form stakes
- flat trowel
- sledgehammer
- wheelbarrow
- pointed trowel
- mason's string
- level or transit
- masonry chisel
- brick mason's jointer
- safety glasses, ear protectors
- masonry wet saw (optional)

Organizing the stones Have the stones delivered as close to the location of the wall as possible to minimize moving. Then start sorting the stones into piles. Reserve those with flat surfaces and 90-degree angles for the wall's most visible surfaces, including the corners and top course. Use less attractive and more oddly shaped rocks as rubble to fill the interior of the wall.

1 To keep frost heave or soil movement from affecting the wall, a stable foundation is essential. Excavate a trench along the path of the wall to below the frostline, or at least 18 inches deep. Dig the trench at least 6 inches wider than the wall will be (22 inches, in this case), then fill it with crushed stone. Tamp the stone flat with a gas-powered plate compactor.

Next, make a concrete form along each side of the trench. Rip ¼-inch-thick hardboard or plywood into 4-inch-wide strips and stake them horizontally around the perimeter of the trench to create a form. The thin material will easily bend to accommodate curves in the wall. Support the forms with stakes every 12 inches or so, leaving them in place until the concrete sets. Mix a batch of concrete and spread it to fill the form. Smooth the surface, then press ½-inch-diameter rebar of an appropriate length halfway down into the concrete. Slightly overlap the bars as necessary so that they run the length of the wall. Insert three lengths of rebar, spaced evenly across the width of the foundation.

2 Mix one sack of mortar in a wheelbarrow and park it near the foundation. Set the first stone into place with its flattest side facing out along one side of the wood form. Use a small sledgehammer to tap the stone into the damp concrete of the foundation, as shown. Pick up some mortar with a trowel and spread a thick layer onto the end of the stone. Select another flat stone and position it end to end against the first one. Ideally, the joints between stones will be closely spaced and consistent in width. If there's a gap between two stones, you can fill it with a small rock later. Continue to set stones, alternately working the two sides of the wall. When necessary, mix another batch of mortar.

tip: work quickly
On a long wall, be careful not to pour more concrete in the form than you can work with before it sets. Leave the rebar sticking out of the concrete at the end of the pour.

4 As you approach the top of the wall, drive two wooden stakes into the ground at each end and at the center. Stretch a nylon string between the stakes at the desired height of the wall, as shown. To ensure that the string is perfectly level, use a line level (which attaches to the string), a builder's level, or a transit.

Topping off the wall For the wall's top surface, use the flat stones separated from the pile that have at least one straight, relatively square edge. Spread a thick layer of mortar across the rubble and carefully set each "cap" stone into place, with its flat side facing up and its straight edge facing out. Make sure you fill and compact mortar in all the joints. Then, with the trowel handle, lightly tap each stone down into the mortar until it's aligned with the string.

3 Once you complete the first courses along the front and back sides of the wall, use a pointed trowel to apply mortar across the joints on the backs of the stones. Also fill in any narrow voids between the stones. Put a big dollop of mortar onto smaller rocks and push them into any large gaps you find between two stones.

Fill the interior space between the front and rear walls with rubble—the less useable stones picked out of the pile. Set each course of stones into a bed of mortar. Every now and then, take a long stone and lay it across the width of the wall so that it extends through to the other side. These crosstie stones will add stability to the wall as it grows in height.

Now spread mortar across the top of the first course and set another course on top of it. Again, be sure that the flattest surfaces face out and that the stones fit closely together. If necessary, place small stone slivers, called chinks, between stones to hold them upright and to prevent them from wobbling. Continue to fill the interior with mortar and rubble. Then remove the wood forms and stakes from the base of the wall.

tip: stagger joints
For superior strength, always stagger the stones so that the joints never form a straight line or cross-shaped intersection. Follow the formula "2 over 1, 1 over 2."

5

6

tip: vary sizes It's tempting to use the largest stones along the base to save lifting them to higher courses. Instead, build the first course out of various-size stones— not just the largest ones. You'll end up with a more natural-looking wall.

5 Work your way along the top of the wall, setting the stones as close together as possible. If necessary, use a small sledgehammer and masonry chisel to chop a stone down to size.

6 Allow the mortar to cure for an hour or so, depending on the weather, then use a brick mason's jointer to strike (smooth out) the joints. Next, inspect both sides of the wall for any empty joints or spaces between the stones, and fill any gaps with fresh mortar.

pergola

Pergola or arbor? The difference is rather like "tomayto," "tomahto." An arbor is typically made of rustic wood or latticework on which plants, such as climbing shrubs or vines, are grown. A pergola uses posts or columns to support a trelliswork roof for climbing plants to grow on.

materials and tools

- two 4-inch-diameter steel posts, 9 feet long (or two 6-by-6 wooden posts, 14 feet long)
- one beam, 6-by-10 rough-cut cedar, 16 feet long
- eight crosspieces, 3-by-8 rough-cut cedar, 5 feet long
- five rails, 2-by-2 rough-cut cedar, 16 feet long
- cardboard and plywood for pattern
- eight ½-inch-diameter lag screws, 8 inches long, with flat washers
- marine adhesive
- hot-dipped galvanized nails or vinyl-coated screws, 3 inches long
- eight ½-inch-diameter lag screws, 6 inches long
- four ¾-inch-diameter hardwood dowels
- jigsaw (or band saw)
- crushed rock (for posts)
- tape measure
- circular saw
- hammer and drill
- chisel
- framing square
- level
- chalk line

A pergola covered with roses, grapes, or flowering vines not only can be a pleasant garden retreat but can serve as an entryway to a courtyard or garden. It can also provide shade on a narrow and little-used side of the house.

The 9-foot-tall pergola shown here, built by This Old House master carpenter Norm Abram, links the house to a nearby guesthouse. The structure, which rests on two 4-inch-diameter steel posts, was built with rough-cut cedar that is naturally resistant to bugs and decay; it also could have been built from redwood or pressure-treated wood. The pergola's overhead structure consists of a 16-foot-long 6-by-10 beam. The eight crosspieces are 5-foot-long 3 by 8s, and the seven top rails are 2 by 2s. (If 3 by 8s are not available, substitute 4 by 8s.)

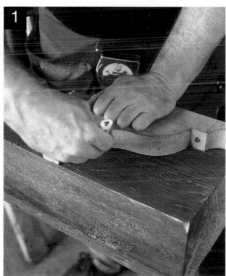

1 For the decorative ends of the beam and crosspieces, make a cardboard pattern similar to the one shown (or your own design); transfer it to a piece of plywood

and cut it out with a jigsaw. Use it as a pattern to mark the ends of the beam and crosspieces. Cut the pattern on the ends of the beam and crosspieces with a jigsaw or a band saw. In this case, Norm anchored the beam and the outriggers on a workbench and then pushed the band saw—mounted on casters—through the wood.

2 On the top of the beam, mark 16-inch centers for the crosspieces and then fit the beam and the 3-by-8 crosspieces together with lap joints in each. To do this, first cut a series of 1½-inch-deep kerfs in the beam with a circular saw. Use a chisel to remove the remaining material. Cut a matching 1½-inch-deep lap in the center of the crosspiece and chisel out the space until the two pieces fit smoothly together.

4

In the beam, drill a corresponding ³⁄₈-inch-diameter hole 3¹⁄₂ inches deep at each crosspiece. To assemble the structure, apply marine adhesive to the lap joints, and then insert an 8-inch-long, ¹⁄₂-inch-diameter lag screw from the top of each crosspiece through the beam. There's no need to plug the counterbores at the top of the crosspieces, because the 2-by-2 rails will cover them.

3

3 Before attaching the crosspieces to the beam, use a framing square to check that the crosspieces are square to the beam and that the sides of the joint are straight. With a sharp chisel, flatten any irregularities in the lap joints until the two pieces fit together like Lincoln Logs.

4 The crosspieces are attached to the beam with marine adhesive and lag screws. Starting from the top of each crosspiece directly above the lap joints, drill a 1¹⁄₂-inch-diameter counterbore 2 inches deep. Then drill a ¹⁄₂-inch-diameter hole all the way through the crosspiece.

5

5 Space the 2-by-2 top rails evenly across the crosspieces and allow the ends to run long. Then fasten them to the crosspieces with marine adhesive and 3-inch hot-dipped galvanized nails or vinyl-coated screws. After the rails are installed, measure for a 3-inch overhang at each end, snap a chalk line across them, and cut with a circular saw.

6 It took Norm and seven helpers to mount the heavy pergola on the two steel posts, then they locked it in place with eight 6-inch lag screws. To better blend with the garden and house, the supporting posts were later turned into what appear to be stone columns once covered with faux stone.

Using alternate posts An alternative approach to using steel posts is to mount the pergola on two 6-by-6 posts set at least 4 feet into the ground (contact your local building inspector for approval). Space the posts so that they will fall between the second and third crosspieces from each end. Steel brackets can be used to connect the posts to the beam, but Norm's recommendation, shown in

the illustration at left, is just as strong and looks much cleaner. He recommends first notching the bottom of the beam 1 inch deep to fit over the top of the posts. Then he suggests creating a tenon on each post and corresponding mortises in the beam. Make the mortises 3 inches square and 6 inches deep and centered on the notch; make the tenons centered on the top of the post, 3 inches square and $5\frac{7}{8}$ inches long. Finally, connect the posts to the beam with marine adhesive and two $\frac{3}{4}$-inch-diameter hardwood dowels through each tenon.

PERGOLA WITH WOOD BEAM POSTS

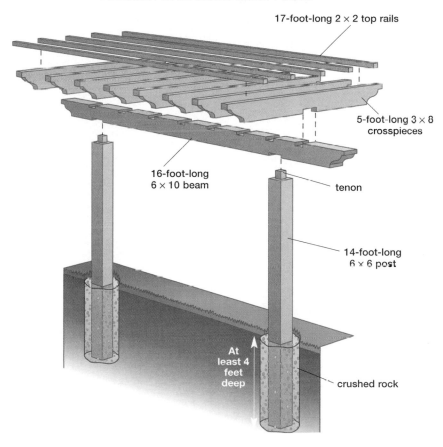

17-foot-long 2 × 2 top rails

5-foot-long 3 × 8 crosspieces

16-foot-long 6 × 10 beam

tenon

14-foot-long 6 × 6 post

At least 4 feet deep

crushed rock

picket fence

The key to building a strong and lasting wood fence is to make it straight and set the posts well. The rest is mostly a matter of design and basic carpentry.

Because a fence establishes a line of division, it is considerate to discuss your plans and the fence style with your neighbors before you begin building. If your fence will run along a shared property line, one or more of the neighbors might split the cost with you if the fence is also attractive to their needs.

A fence's primary components are vertical posts and horizontal rails. What makes each fence unique is the type of boards used and the way they are applied. Some typical materials for wood fences include pickets, vertical or horizontal boards, boards and battens, lattice-topped boards, and rails.

Top lumber choices for fence materials are decay-resistant wood, such as heart cedar and redwood. Pressure-treated wood, such as southern yellow pine, also serves well, but it tends to warp and crack after a few years. In addition, pressure-treated wood does not accept paint and stain well.

Increasingly popular are fences made from recycled materials. Recycled plastic or fiberglass-reinforced plastic fences neither crack nor need painting, making them maintenance

free. However, they are not as strong as wood.

The 4-foot-high picket fence shown here was built from a kit that uses 8-foot-long pre-assembled wood picket panels and 6-by-6 cedar posts that were factory mortised. All are fabricated from white cedar.

Before you start building, check first with your public utilities office for the locations of any buried water or gas lines. Also locate where the first and last posts will be and then adjust as much as possible so the panels can be installed without having to be shortened.

materials and tools

- ■ fence kit that includes 6-by-6 posts and pre-assembled wood picket panels
- ■ vinyl-coated fence screws
- ■ crushed rock (for posts)
- ■ ready-mix concrete (for gateposts)
- ■ gate hinges and latch
- ■ posthole digger
- ■ circular saw
- ■ level or fence-post level
- ■ shovel
- ■ tamping bar
- ■ stakes
- ■ mason's string
- ■ cordless drill

ANATOMY OF A PICKET FENCE

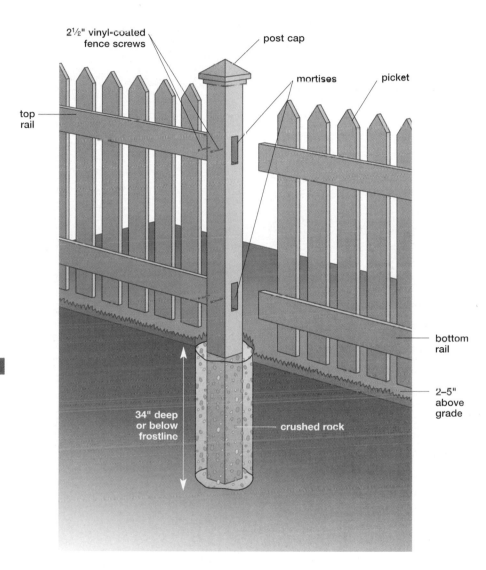

2½" vinyl-coated fence screws

post cap

mortises

picket

top rail

bottom rail

34" deep or below frostline

crushed rock

2–5" above grade

1 For these 6-by-6 posts, the hole should be 10 inches in diameter, to leave 2 inches all around for the tamping bar. With a posthole digger, dig the hole approximately 34 inches deep and then add 2 inches of crushed rock as a drain. To position the bottom of the pickets 2 to 5 inches above the ground, adjust the post height by adding or removing some rock.

3 Put a screw in the outside face of the post 5 inches above the ground and run mason's string to a stake driven at the end of the fence or at the first corner. Pull the string taut and wrap it around the stake 5 inches above grade. The string must be flush with the outer face of the post. From the first post, measure out the length of the fence panel and dig the next hole there. Put the post in the hole, but do not set it until the fence panel is installed.

4 Slide the fence panel rails into the mortises of the first post and then into the mortises on the second post, which is still loose in the posthole. Be sure the second post is plumb in all directions. Use wedges under the panel to adjust its height. When correct, set the post, continuing to check for plumb in both directions. When this post

and all successive ones are set, the outer face of each post should just touch the string. If the wind is blowing, watch that it does not push the string out of line. Double-check your work as you proceed by taking a few moments to sight down the posts, ensuring that the tops are all in line and not leaning in or out.

2 Set the post in the hole. While a helper holds a level on the post to keep it plumb, shovel in 4 to 5 inches of crushed rock around the post; the rock packs well and drains better than soil. Tamp the material thoroughly, then add another layer and tamp that. If working alone, use a fence-post level that straps to the post.

5

7

important step for a professional look. After the post is set, drive two vinyl-coated screws through the back of the post and into the rails.

5 When you are building a fence on sloping ground, the panel can be racked so that the pickets will remain vertical even as the fence rises steadily or moves down the hill. To make the panel flexible, lift it as shown and drop one rail on a block of wood, then repeat on the opposite end. You may have to do this several times until the panel gives and can be adjusted. Install the panel between posts as described, keeping the bottoms of the pickets consistent in height with other panels.

6

6 Place each panel between the posts, but before you set the next post, adjust it so that the space between the post and the nearest picket is equal to the picket spacing. This adjustment often involves only an inch or two, but it's an

7 Because gateposts take abuse from the opening and closing gate, set them in ready-mix concrete for greater stability. Space the gateposts the width of the gate plus 1½ inches. Double-check that the posts are level and plumb and that the second post is in line with the string. Also check the spacing between the gatepost and the nearest picket, adjusting as necessary.

8 The gate generally matches the fence, but it can also be different to draw attention to itself. Position the gate between the posts and support each end on wedges. The gate should have a ¾-inch clearance on each side so it can open without hitting the post. Screw strap hinges from the post to the top and bottom rails of the gate. On slopes, put the hinges on the uphill post. Remove the wedges, check that the gate swings smoothly, then install the latch.

8

pond and waterfall

A pond, stream, or waterfall can turn even a small garden into a relaxing escape zone that is seemingly far from worldly intrusions. By using some purchased components and basic how-to skills, you can create nature in your own backyard.

Sloping ground is perfect for a stream and waterfall, but building up flat ground can also create the right terrain. Either way, take your time in deciding where to place a water feature. It may be in a little-used and out-of-the-way section of garden. It may also be where it becomes the focal point of your whole yard. If so, position it so it can be enjoyed from a porch, patio, or deck, as well as from indoors.

When deciding on a location, consider nearby trees and the amount of sunshine. Try to avoid placing the pond close to trees, because the excavation will damage the roots. Also, tree litter that falls into the pond will require regular skimming to prevent vegetation from sinking to the bottom and decomposing. And make sure the pond receives adequate sunshine too, as many water plants need at least 6 hours of direct sunlight each day.

planning

Before embarking on building your own water feature, be sure to understand the basic components.

Pumps Garden pond pumps are necessary to circulate water through filters and to a waterfall or fountain.

Submersible pumps are virtually silent and have extra-long power cords to reach from the bottom of the pond to the nearest electrical outlet.

Surface, or inline, pumps are more powerful and energy efficient than submersible pumps, but they are noisier and must not be submerged. They are normally located near the pond, but hidden in a small structure.

Combination inline and submersible pumps, which operate equally well underwater or on land, are frequently used in water gardens because of their flexibility.

The pump should circulate the entire volume of the pond each hour. If you're building a waterfall, the pump must be sized to pump the same volume of water from the lowest point of the pond to the top of the waterfall.

Filters Pond filters are either mechanical or biological. A mechanical filter catches solid debris, but it does not remove waste that is toxic to fish. If you want fish, a biological filter is also essential. For smaller ponds with fish, a biological filter alone will suffice.

Valves In a pond system, different types of valves have different uses.

A float valve maintains a constant water level in the pond, replacing water lost to evaporation and leaks as needed. A check valve is a fitting that allows water to flow only in one direction. Check valves are normally attached to the discharge side of the pump to prevent water going to the waterfall or the top of the stream from draining back down the pipe when the pump is off.

Gate valves are normally either completely open or closed, although they can also be used to control water flow. They are excellent for a leakproof water shutoff.

tip: child safety

If small children in your household or neighborhood can wander into the garden, the pond needs to be fenced, whether or not local ordinances require it. A toddler who trips and falls into a pond or stream can drown in just a few inches of water. An alternative to a permanent fence is a portable one that can be put up when you are not in the immediate area.

Ball valves open or close with just a half-turn of the handle. They are excellent for controlling water flow, such as when you want to reduce the flow to a waterfall or stream. Less expensive models, however, may not completely shut off the water.

Piping The most popular piping or tubing materials for ponds and waterfalls are flexible PVC, corrugated black vinyl (the interior is smooth), and rigid PVC. For piping water underground from the source to your pond, rigid PVC pipe is the best choice. In and around the pond, stream, and waterfall, however, flexible PVC and corrugated black vinyl are more practical, because they can readily be bent around, over, and under obstacles.

Pond liners The standard pond liner is 45-mil EPDM, a synthetic rubber that is flexible, easy to work with, and resistant to chemicals and ultraviolet rays. Always use fish-safe EPDM and not the kind used for roofing material, which contains toxic chemicals. The liner comes in a variety of widths and lengths.

Other pond liners include butyl rubber, which is similar to EPDM but harder to find and more expensive; black PVC, which is easily punctured and disintegrates when exposed to sunlight; and polyethylene, which is resistant to chemicals but stiff and difficult to work with.

All pond liners need a protective underlayment to minimize the chance of punctures from rocks and roots. The under-layment can be purchased where you buy the liner, but old carpet or carpet pad works equally well.

It's better to have too much liner than too little. To estimate your needs, measure the pond's length and width. To each measurement, add three times the pool depth. As an example, a pool 15 feet long, 10 feet wide, and 3 feet deep would need a liner 19 feet wide (3×3 feet deep = 9, added to the 10-foot width) and 24 feet long (3×3 feet deep = 9, added to the 15-foot length).

Reservoirs If you plan to have a stream or waterfall with your pond, place a reservoir at the top. This can be nothing more than a vinyl bucket, but one made specifically for your purpose is easier to install and connect to the piping. Some manufactured waterfall reservoirs are designed with a biological filter and a special lip to create a pleasing shape.

Reservoirs are also essential for a stream with no waterfall or pond. The water emerges from rocks at the upper end, as if from a spring in the ground, and disappears into the

RIGID PVC

CORRUGATED BLACK VINYL

SIZING PIPE

The amount of water that can be moved through a pipe depends in part on the water pressure, but mostly on the pipe size, which is measured according to its interior diameter. Use this guide in planning your water feature.

PIPE SIZE	GALLONS PER HOUR (MAX)
½ inch	240
1 inch	720
1½ inches	1,320
2 inches	3,000

ground at the low end. A reservoir at this downstream end contains a pump that circulates the water.

Skimmers These are a key to keeping a garden pond free of floating debris. A skimmer is essentially a box with an opening on the side facing the pond. The pump in the skimmer draws water across the surface and through the opening, bringing leaves and other debris with it. The debris is caught in a net inside the skimmer, and then the cleaned water is pumped to a biological filter, waterfall, or fountain. Some skimmers also contain float valves.

Chlorine and chloramine Most water districts add chlorine to water to purify it, but the shift is now to chloramine, which is considered more efficient. Chloramine, however, is toxic to fish and reptiles. Check with your local water supplier to determine if your water contains chloramine. If so, and you are keeping fish, you must use a detoxifier available from pet-supply stores.

materials and tools

- pond and stream underlayment
- pond and stream liner material (45-mil EPDM)
- crushed rock, to support waterfall reservoir and skimmer box
- rocks of varying sizes for lining stream and waterfall
- washed drain rock for streambed
- 90° elbow, couplings, gate valve, T-fitting to connect to water source
- GFCI-protected 120-volt outlet
- waterfall reservoir
- reservoir water-supply pipe
- flexible PVC pipe to connect skimmer to waterfall
- check valve
- rope or garden hose

- landscaper's spray paint
- pipe wrenches
- pointed and square-nose shovels
- mattock
- wheelbarrow
- hammer
- tape measure
- hand tamper
- 4-foot level
- line level or water level
- small stakes
- pure silicone caulk and caulking gun, or black expanding foam
- eye protection
- water plants, shrubs, and flowers
- diamond-tipped blade in a circular saw for cutting rock (optional)

ANATOMY OF A WATERFALL, STREAM, AND POND

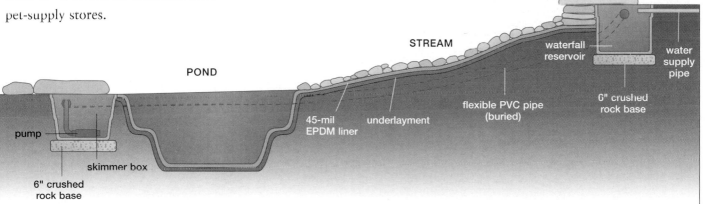

WATERFALL

STREAM

POND

waterfall reservoir

water supply pipe

flexible PVC pipe (buried)

6" crushed rock base

45-mil EPDM liner

underlayment

pump

skimmer box

6" crushed rock base

1 Experiment with different shapes for the waterfall, stream, and pond by using a garden hose or rope to mark the outlines. In outlining the stream, plan several curves, rapids, and falls into small pools en route to the pond. Sketch each new outline and consider your choices over a few days. Once you have decided, mark the final shape with landscaper's spray paint.

2 The easiest way to bring water to the pond is to tap into the nearest outside spigot, or hose bib. No cutting is necessary. To do this, turn off the house water supply and unscrew the hose bib. Use two pipe wrenches, one to turn the hose bib and

the other to prevent the pipe from turning. In this case, a 90° elbow was installed on the end of the pipe, followed by threaded couplings on each side of a gate valve, then a T-fitting, with one outlet going to the hose bib and the other to the pond's water-supply pipe. The gate valve allows the homeowner to shut off water to the pond for repairs without closing down the household water. Additionally, a GFCI-protected 120-volt outlet is necessary to

power the pump. Electrical code requires that the outlet be at least 10 feet from the water feature.

3 Find a place at the top of the stream for the waterfall reservoir. It should be positioned on a spot no more than one-third the elevation between the pond at the bottom of the stream and the base of the waterfall. Dig the hole until the waterfall is at the desired height, then dig down another 6 inches and fill that with crushed rock. Use a hand tamper to pack it firmly. At this point, install the water-supply pipe connection and pipe to the back of the box. Use a 4-foot level to confirm that the reservoir is perfectly level side to side and tilted forward until the bubble is about ¼ off center. Once the reservoir is positioned, backfill around it with the excavated soil and tamp it firmly as you proceed. Having someone stand in the reservoir during the backfilling process will further stabilize the box. Check the level repeatedly to ensure the reservoir does not move.

Excavation Begin digging the pond just inside the outline and remove 8 to 10 inches of soil. Then place a long, straight 2 by 4 across the opening on edge with a level taped to it, to determine how level the pond perimeter is. Check from several angles. Adjust the perimeter height as needed by digging down the high side or adding soil to the low side. Then use landscaper's paint to mark the first plant shelf, which should be 8 to 12 inches wide and extend all around the pond. In the area beyond this first shelf, dig down another 8 to 10 inches where the second shelf will be. Then stop and determine exactly where the water level will be. Pick a spot 2 inches below the top of the excavation and use a line level or water level to determine where the pond's surface will be all around the excavation. Mark it with a series of small stakes. Check the depth of the plant shelves again and adjust as necessary. Then dig out the remainder of the pond.

4 Dig out an area for the skimmer box at the pond's edge. Set the box on a packed base of crushed rock (about 6 inches) so it won't settle. Position it so the water level in the box will be ¾ inch below the top of its opening leading into the pond. Ensure that the box is perfectly level from side to side and front to back. Connect the flexible PVC pipe to the back of the skimmer according to the model's directions. Place the pump in the skimmer box.

Install the pond liner around the face of the skimmer according to the accompanying directions. Finally, fit a check valve to the pump's discharge side.

5 Working from the top down, install rocks of varying sizes along the streambed to outline the shape and reinforce the banks. Add more soil as necessary to build up the lower side of stream curves to prevent water from washing over the top. Deepen the streambed at sharp curves as necessary to keep the water contained. Fill gaps between large rocks with 2-inch or larger washed drain rock. The liner will fit over the built-up soil embankments, and the larger rocks will both anchor the liner and be an integral part of the stream.

HOW BIG A POND?

If you plan to have just a few goldfish, the minimum water depth for their well-being is 18 to 20 inches. If you plan to raise koi, which can grow to 2 feet in length, you'll need a pond at least 3 to 4 feet deep. In areas where the surface can freeze, make the pond 24 to 30 inches deep for any kind of fish.

Check local ordinances for allowable depth and square footage and for fencing requirements.

Lots of water is needed to fill a pond, but once it's filled, you'll only need to replace losses from leaks or evaporation. To estimate how much water your pond will need, use the following formula. Be sure to convert all measurements to feet. For instance, 9 inches is 0.75 foot and 18 inches is 1.5 feet.

- Rectangular or square pond: length × width × depth × 7.5 = gallons

- Circular pond: diameter squared × depth × 5.9 = gallons

- Oval pond: length × width × depth × 6.7 = gallons

For an irregular outline, divide the shape into a series of rectangles or squares, calculate the volume for each, and add together.

6 Lay the flexible PVC pipe (in this case, 2-inch diameter) between the waterfall reservoir and the pump in the skimmer. The supply pipe can be buried in the streambed or run up the side of the garden, as here, depending on convenience. Bury the pipe 6 inches to prevent accidental damage to it.

6

7

7 Starting from the top, pull the under-layment across the streambed and pond and fit it to the excavation as you work down the slope. Add extra cushioning over any sharp rocks or roots that could not be removed. Fit the underlayment as smoothly as possible and then install the liner in the same manner. Folds and wrinkles are unavoidable, but smooth them as best you can. Most creases will eventually be hidden by the rock lining. Allow ample amounts of liner on both sides of the stream for later adjustments.

8 After pulling the stream liner up to the front of the reservoir and attaching it according to that brand's directions, begin installing rocks around the box to hide it. When possible, mix large and small rocks for a more natural appearance. Place the largest rocks on each side of the waterfall's box to frame it, and then build up the center section. Rocks can be glued to each other and to the EPDM liner with pure silicone caulk or black expanding foam sold at pond-supply outlets. The foam is useful to fill gaps between large rocks. Once the foam is injected, press gravel and sand into the foam to disguise it.

8

thrive in water no deeper than 12 inches. On the second shelf, place baskets of water lilies. As well as oxygenating the pond, plants help maintain the water at an even temperature. About half the pond surface should be covered with plants to provide shade for the fish.

9 Many waterfall reservoirs are equipped with a plastic lip to form the waterfall, but for a better appearance, fit a wide, flat rock to the lip and hold it in place with ample amounts of pure silicone caulk. How far out the stone extends will determine the type of falls you have. For a direct plunge, extend the lip over the pool. Shorten the extension if you want the water to splash down and over rocks that are supporting the waterfall.

10 The final—and best—part of any water garden project is adding a selection of plants, shrubs, and flowers. The choice is wide but will be dictated in part by your climate. In the pond itself, the top shelf is primarily for bog plants that

STREAMS

Streambeds are typically 2 to 4 feet wide and 6 inches to 1 foot deep. As in nature, wider and shallower streambeds indicate slow-moving water, while swifter water is contained in narrower and deeper streambeds. Adjust your stream to your terrain and remember to vary the width. For the steeper stream shown here, several twists and turns were added, along with several small waterfalls that spill into shallow pools. The changing directions of the stream add dynamic interest to the water feature, and the small pools will contain much of the stream when the supply pump is shut off. Along the edge of your stream and occasionally in the middle, excavate a few deeper holes. After the liner is in place, put a number of larger rocks in these holes so that water will naturally swirl around and over them.

patio fountain

The sound of splashing or running water casts a peaceful spell on a patio or an outdoor seating area, and at the same time masks intrusive noises such as traffic or neighbors. Fountains that provide gentle water sounds, such as this freestanding model, come in all sizes and shapes and in a wide variety of materials, including stone, marble, concrete, cast bronze, copper, aluminum, and plastic. Pottery outlets and home-supply centers carry a large number of planters and vases that can be turned into fountains.

Spray and spill are the two basic types of fountains. Spray patterns are controlled by a type of fountain jet, which is attached to a submersible pump. Numerous spray patterns are available, including multiple tiers, circles, geysers, tulip or mushroom shaped, and a bubbler. Some fountain jets are also adjustable. Spill fountains are designed so that water falls into one or more containers, or simply runs over the top of an attractively glazed pot and into a basin under it.

This particular model, with the water splashing down an ornamental sculpture, is a form of spill fountain, but with a different jet it could be converted to a spray fountain.

Fountains are most commonly powered by small 120-volt pumps, but increasingly popular are low-voltage pumps, which make the installation process less risky. A homeowner with no electrical wiring skills can easily connect a low-voltage pump to a transformer circuit. Not all hardware and home-supply centers carry or are aware of low-voltage pumps, but you can find and order them online (see page 184).

- ready-made patio fountain with submersible light
- low-voltage transformers with timer: one for fountain pump, one for submersible lamp
- 12-gauge wire
- heat-shrink electrical tubing connectors
- black electrical tape
- string
- spade
- wire strippers
- wire cutters or lineman's pliers

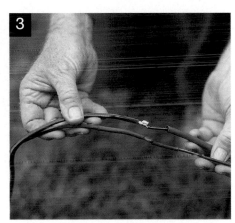

1 The simplest method to run wire to a fountain pump is to use a low-voltage wiring system. If a low-voltage pump is not available in your area, order it online. Wiring that must cross a lawn can be buried without significantly disturbing the sod. Stretch a length of string to guide you, and then cut a 5-inch-deep slit with a spade. Push the handle over to widen the cut as you go. Follow this by pressing the wire into the slit with a stick. After the wire is buried, simply press the sod back together with your foot and the cut disappears.

2 Position the transformer on a wall or wood stake beside the house. Transformers should be at least 12 inches above the ground. The larger transformer with a timer shown here is for the fountain pump; the other is for a submersible lamp. Use multipurpose wire strippers to expose ½ inch of bare copper from the ends of the two 12-gauge wires. Ensure that the transformer is not plugged in, then wrap the stripped ends of the wires around the transformer's contact screws and tighten.

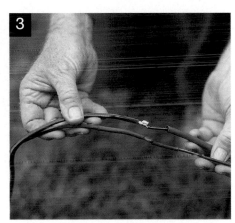

3 Low-voltage pumps commonly come with an electrical cord and plug. When there is no nearby low-voltage outlet available, as in this case, simply cut off the plug and strip the insulation back 1 inch on both wires. Do the same on the wires coming from the transformer, then make the connection watertight with heat-shrink

electrical tubing, available in most hardware or home-supply stores. Slip the tubing over one wire, twist the exposed ends tightly together, and then wrap the wire with black electrical tape (not shown here so the connection can be seen). Slide the shrink tubing over the connection and heat with a match or lighter until it pulls tightly around the connection. Be careful not to overheat the wires and melt the insulation in the process.

4 Run the wiring for the pump and underwater light through the hole in the bottom of the basin. The wires fit into the center of a special rubber plug normally available from the fountain supplier. Slip the wires into the plug, fit the plug into the basin hole, and then seal around the plug with pure silicone caulk. Finally, connect a short length of tubing from the pump to the fountain, fill the basin with water, and plug the transformer into a GFCI-protected outlet. If the pump does not begin operating immediately, check the timing setting on the transformer.

CHAPTER FIVE

plants

THEY MAKE OUR LANDSCAPES COME ALIVE,
ADDING DELIGHTFUL COLORS, TEXTURES, AND SCENTS

AWARE OF IT OR NOT, WE ALL RESPOND TO PLANTS. Though it's the structures—the house, walkways, decks, and porches—that define outdoor spaces, plants and the way they are combined create the sense of beauty and unity that a pleasing landscape requires. Trees, shrubs, ground covers, vines, and lawns are used to create outdoor spaces that are comfortable, appealing, and engaging.

But landscape styles and trends change over time. For instance, a generation ago, the favored look was cubed or balled plants lined up singly around a house. Today, plants are massed less formally, in groupings that need less pruning yet are visually strong. Their shapes, textures, and colors are employed to highlight the architectural features of a home.

In this chapter, you'll learn more about the roles permanent plants play in the landscape and how to plant them and keep them healthy. Starting on page 153, lists of plants for various uses offer a guide to choosing the best ones for different situations. For information about lawn planting and care, see page 176.

landscaping with plants

Before you begin narrowing your plant choices, take an objective look at your house and yard and make a list of how plants can best be used in your landscape. The challenge is to arrange plants to show off their best qualities while making sure they also complement each other and your house. Following are some of the aesthetic and practical benefits of different kinds of plants.

Trees Large or small, every garden needs trees for shading, screening, and shelter. Trees are the backbone of the landscape, and because of their size they have more impact than most other plants. Maybe you're lucky and your garden already includes the trees you need. If not, then carefully choose and plant them before any other plants.

Some trees display colorful flowers, berries, or beautiful fall foliage (or all three). Smaller trees create an understory—an intermediate link between larger trees and lower-growing shrubs—that gives the landscape more depth.

Evergreens provide winter color and shelter for birds; they also can be used to block wind and provide privacy year-round. Deciduous trees bring cooling shade in summer, then shed their leaves to allow the sun's warmth in winter. Properly sited to the west and south of the house, they can reduce heating and cooling costs.

ABOVE: Young sour gum trees with orange fall foliage, a sheared evergreen hedge in back, and mounding azaleas in front combine for a layered effect with lots of color variation.
LEFT: Trees, shrubs, vines, and perennials transform a basic deck into an inviting retreat. Purple and variegated foliage provides much of the color accent.

Shrubs It's difficult to imagine a landscape without shrubs, because they are so varied, offer so much beauty, and solve so many problems. Shrubs add seasonal color with foliage, flowers, and fruit. They soften foundations and the edges of decks, porches, and doorways. They also are well suited for hedges that define space, provide privacy, and screen unsightly views. Though shrubs are not as imposing as shade trees, many will live as long and can be just as important in your landscape.

Lawns and ground covers
A large expanse of lawn is part of most home landscapes because it's pleasing to the eye, soft underfoot, durable, and versatile enough to serve many roles. Above all, lawns are the exemplary surface for play.

However, lawns require a lot of watering, cutting, and care, and alternatives are catching on. In the dry West, tough, drought-tolerant grasses, such as buffalo and blue grama, make more sense than traditional Kentucky bluegrass. And every region has a range of low ground covers that mimic the green expanses of traditional lawns but do not demand as much water and maintenance. Choose a ground cover that suits your climate and landscape situation: for sun, shade, a slope, to

Mountain laurels, thriving in the filtered shade of tall trees, are well positioned to screen the deck from neighbors' views. The spring-flowering shrubs are evergreen.

take foot traffic, for foliage only, or for flowers and fruit.

Perennials With their colorful flowers and foliage, perennials attract attention over a long season. Depending on your taste and style, you may want these plants to provide broad sweeps of bright, long-lasting color throughout the landscape, or you may prefer more subdued plantings with occasional splashes of color fading in and out. To extend the flowering period in all parts of your landscape, intersperse perennials with flowering shrubs.

Vines Vines are like jewelry: they wrap, encircle, adorn, and sometimes dazzle. They are versatile and play a variety of roles, as colorful bowers announcing entryways, softening a wall with greenery, screening unsightly views with evergreen leaves, and creating privacy by covering a trellis. Vines tie together plants of different heights, carrying the eye vertically from low-growing kinds up into the branches of trees.

Summer-blooming yellow coreopsis and bronzy gaillardia mingle in a ribbon of color that makes the transition from lawn to a less formal landscape beyond.

choosing plants

How do you choose one plant over another? Criteria are essential, so start by rejecting plants that don't do well in your growing conditions. Then consider plant appearance, individually and with other plants.

Palo verde provides light shade; penstemon, desert milkweed, and other shrubby perennials attract hummingbirds and butterflies in dry, Southwestern yards.

Viburnums do well in the partial shade of this woodland border (left). All viburnums have attractive flowers, and many kinds, including 'Wentworth' cranberry bush (above), also enhance the garden with bright fall foliage and colorful winter fruit.

Generally, you can assume that reputable nurseries and garden centers in your area offer only plants that are well adapted to your climate. But this isn't always true at big, national home-center chains (or mail-order houses), so be mindful of hardiness and the particular needs of plants in your region.

Climate Plants will thrive in your landscape only if they are adapted to your climate. Adaptability hinges on a variety of factors, but your area's average winter low temperature is critical. (Check for this temperature with the nearest cooperative extension office.) The average winter low temperature is the criterion by which most plants are rated and is the one used in this book.

Size Use the ultimate spread of any plant to determine how far apart to space it from another plant or a structure. If a shrub will spread to 10 feet across, allow at least 5 feet from its trunk to the edge of another plant or a wall, fence, or path. Add another couple of feet near your house so that painting, for instance, is possible. Extra space also helps keep the siding and foundation dry. When spacing plants, err on the generous side, as plants in a good garden situation often grow larger than is typical.

Exposure Place plants where they will get the amount of light they need for optimal growth. Full sun means 6 or more hours of direct sunshine; less than that and you are dealing with partial sun (3 to 6 hours) or full shade (3 hours or less of direct sun).

Water You will always need to water new plantings, and sometimes even established landscapes during prolonged dry spells. However, ideally, a well established landscape, even in a dry region, is only minimally dependent on irrigation.

Soils Most landscape plants adapt to a variety of garden soils, but most need slightly acid soil and modest amounts of organic matter. (For ways to amend soil and make marginally deficient soils more favorable, see page 145.) But if your soil is extreme (very acidic or very alkaline, for instance), look first to plants that are naturally adapted to it.

Pests Each area of the country has its own set of common insect and disease problems, and some plants are particularly susceptible. Before you choose a plant, find out if it is prone to any pests.

plant appearance

Good looks count, but not just in the nursery on the day you shop. Go shopping armed with the specific characteristics of the plants you need. That will narrow the field considerably, making choices simpler. Here are some of the key ornamental characteristics of plants to incorporate into your garden.

Seasons Choose plants with different bloom times so that you'll have something in flower from early spring through fall. Since most plants bloom in spring, keep an eye out for ones that bloom in summer and fall.

But don't focus on flowers alone. Leaves that change colors through the year, interesting bark, and bright berries are welcome when little else is happening.

Colors Color is the most striking plant attribute, and you can use it to create effects that are subtle and restful or loud and playful. Use classic combinations, such as blue and white; pink, blue, and white; or blue and yellow. Or create bolder statements with red, yellow, and orange. Don't forget to use colorful foliage plants in your scheme. Plants with yellow foliage or variegated leaves can make a bold statement in the landscape. To unify the landscape, repeat some colors throughout.

Shapes Plants of different shapes add contrast and interest to your landscape. For instance, place tall, narrow trees and shrubs near those with horizontal branching. Combine flat-topped flowers, such as yarrow; ball-shaped flowers, such as hydrangea; vertical spires, such as delphiniums; loose, airy flowers, such as lady's-mantle; and spiky foliage, such as New Zealand flax.

Dwarf conifers, including creeping yellow junipers, a bright green pine, and blue spruce, provide color contrast throughout the year. Their varied growth habits, from sprawling to upright, also add interest.

start with good soil

The best soil for growing plants is well drained and crumbly, with balanced nutrients and a good supply of organic matter. Before you plant, it's a good idea to test your soil, learn its characteristics, and then improve only those aspects that need it.

soil types

Soils are classified as predominantly sand, clay, or loam. Sandy soils drain well, but since they don't hold water you need to irrigate more frequently. You also need to fertilize more often because sand has few nutrients and doesn't retain many that are added. Clay soil has the opposite properties: high fertility and good water retention, but sometimes too much. Loam soil has the benefits of both sand and clay and the drawbacks of neither.

A free-form berm allows you to add your own well-drained, compost-enriched soil.

testing drainage

The roots of most plants need a constant supply of oxygen from the soil, but poorly draining soil holds so much water that there's little room for oxygen. Many azaleas and dogwoods will die when planted in waterlogged soil, though willows and winterberry thrive in such conditions.

To check drainage, dig a hole 18 inches deep and fill it with water. After it drains, fill it again, and this time note how fast it drains. If the hole drains in an hour or less, the drainage is good. If water remains for several hours or longer, the drainage is poor.

A built-in patio planter filled with improved soil supports birch trees and ground covers.

Options for poor drainage

If drainage is a problem, you have two alternatives: improve the drainage or choose plants that will tolerate soggy soil. (See page 155 for a list of trees that thrive in soggy soils.)

One way to improve drainage is to build mounds or berms, or raised beds. The 6 to 12 inches of well-drained soil these raised planting beds provide is enough for most plants to thrive.

Since not all poor drainage is a matter of soil type, analyze the cause and consider possible solutions. If drainage is a sitewide problem, a piped drainage system may be the answer (see page 70).

soil pH

A soil's pH is a measure of its alkalinity or acidity, and it affects plant growth significantly. The pH scale ranges from 1 (extremely acidic) to 14 (extremely alkaline), with 7 being neutral. But few soils are more acidic than a pH of 5, or more alkaline than a pH of 8. Most plants grow best in slightly acidic soil, one with a pH of 6 to 7. If the pH of your soil is not within this slightly acidic range, some plants will have a difficult time absorbing some nutrients.

Acid soil is common where rainfall is heavy and where soils are sandy or high in organic matter. Though most plants grow well in

Soil test kits typically measure the basics—pH and key nutrients. They work by mixing a small amount of soil with water and comparing the resulting color to the chart provided.

mildly acid soil, too much acidity will inhibit growth. The remedy for soil that is too acidic is limestone (calcium carbonate).

Alkaline soil is typical in regions where rainfall is light, or where the soil is naturally high in lime. While most plants tolerate mildly alkaline soils, certain key nutrients, usually iron, become less available to the plant roots as the soil becomes more alkaline. The remedy for alkaline soils is elemental sulfur.

Notable exceptions to these guidelines, such as azaleas and camellias, need soil that is more acidic than most plants, from 4.5 to 5.5. Lilacs, however, prefer an alkaline soil with a pH greater than 7.0.

The acid-alkaline balance of your soil, called pH, is critical for proper plant growth. To raise pH, add limestone; to lower it, add sulfur.

Generally speaking, soils east of the Mississippi River are acidic, while those in the West are alkaline. But the only way to find out your soil's pH is to have it tested. Do-it-yourself testing kits are available (see page 184 for sources), but the most accurate results come from samples sent to agricultural universities or commercial soil laboratories for analysis.

The pH of your soil and the amounts of clay or sand it includes determine how much lime or sulfur is needed. For how much to add, see the directions that accompany the soil test kit or the report returned by the soil testing laboratory.

the magic of organic matter

Mulch is much cheaper in bulk, by the cubic yard, than it is in bags.

Most new home sites are not the best place to garden. The soil has been through the upheaval of foundation digging followed by compaction from the battalion of heavy building equipment. This process often brings the subsoil to the surface, causing the topsoil to be forever lost and the remaining soil to be forever compacted. Even construction of a deck, patio, or walkway can damage neighboring soil. Rather than expect any plant to grow on a new site, amend poor soils by incorporating as much organic matter as possible into it.

Organic matter can improve any type of soil. It increases the water-holding capacity of sandy soils and improves the drainage of clay soils. It does this by providing food for the many kinds of existing microorganisms, which in turn create structure-enhancing soil humus.

Many types of organic amendments are available, either commercially packaged or sold in bulk. An excellent choice is aged steer manure, which contains more nutrients than most other amendments. Compost is another good choice, whether homemade or purchased. Many cities now compost their green waste rather than bury it, and mushroom compost (a by-product of mushroom farming) is available in many areas.

Be generous when adding organic amendments. When preparing a new planting bed, spread a 2- to 3-inch layer of amendment over the soil and dig or till it into the top 6 to 9 inches.

Around established plantings, add organic material to the soil by spreading it over the soil surface as a mulch; earthworms, microorganisms, and water will help mix it into the soil.

Three-bin compost systems—one bin each for fresh, mid-term, and finished material—are a good source of organic matter.

fertilizers

To grow properly, plants need a steady supply of nutrients, and some of the most important ones come directly from the air and water. But gardeners must provide a few of the others, the most important of which is nitrogen (N). It's primarily responsible for the dark green color of healthy leaves. Other key nutrients often needed by garden plants are phosphorus (P) and potassium (K).

Fast-growing plants, such as grasses and flowering plants, are most likely to need additional fertilizer, while mature trees and shrubs normally need the least. But if you see that plants are not growing well, or that their leaf color is pale and growth is weak, you can assume that something is needed, though it may not be fertilizer. If you haven't already done so, have your soil tested (see page 145) for pH and the availability of basic nutrients.

There are two primary categories of fertilizer: synthetic and natural. Either may be dry or liquid, fast or slow release. Both aid plant growth, but synthetics do less for the health of the soil and the organisms that live in it. If you use a synthetic, replenish the soil's natural fertility by regularly applying compost or organic mulch.

Once you know which nutrients to add, your best guide is the fertilizer label. The three prominent numbers on it, such as 5-10-5, indicate the percentages it contains of the three primary nutrients—N-P-K, always in that order. Therefore, 5-10-5 means the fertilizer contains 5 percent nitrogen, 10 percent phosphorus, and 5 percent potassium. The amount of nitrogen drives the amount to use: apply 1 pound of nitrogen per 1,000 square feet of plantings, the equivalent of 20 pounds of a 5-10-5 product (1 pound divided by 5 percent, or .05).

Fertilizers are also either fast or slow acting. (Actually, the nitrogen they contain acts either quickly or slowly.) Fast-acting types give plants a quick boost, but it's easy to apply too much. Slow-acting fertilizers release nitrogen gradually. Most organic fertilizers are essentially slow acting, though the timing of nutrient release is unpredictable. Controlled-release types combine the predictability of synthetics with the gradual release of organics.

tip: fertilizer timing

■ **TREES AND SHRUBS** In late fall or early spring, spread an 18-6-12 or a 16-8-8 fertilizer underneath and slightly beyond the drip line.

■ **LAWNS** Grass type, region, and maintenance level determine amount and schedule. Use a high-nitrogen lawn fertilizer in which at least half of the nitrogen is slow release. Fertilize once or twice in fall. Fertilize northern grasses again in early spring, southern grasses in midspring.

■ **PERENNIALS** Fertilize in early spring with a 10-10-10; repeat once or twice according to need

Fertilizer options include (clockwise from top left): natural, synthetic, controlled-release synthetic, or liquid natural.

planting garden beds

LEFT: *Till a new weed-free planting site to loosen the soil before adding compost and tilling again. BELOW: Before planting, rake in fertilizer and level the soil.*

On a large planting site, spray-paint lines on top of mulch to indicate the shape and size of smaller planting areas for ground covers.

Whether you are planting a small bed by the front door or replacing an entire front lawn, planning what the area will look like and preparing the soil are key steps.

getting ready to plant

To prepare a new garden bed, first sketch a plan showing the shape and size of the bed and the type and location of each plant. If you have a complete landscape plan, such as the one on page 23, refer to it when laying out beds.

Be sure to choose plants that are compatible with the size and dimensions of the planting area. For example, perennials are a good choice for a 3-foot-wide border. From a lawn or pathway on the edge of the bed, you can comfortably reach plants to weed and water them. Ground cover plants or mixed plantings that include shrubs require more space. (To plant a large shrub from a container, follow the guidelines for tree planting on page 150.) In larger beds, add steppingstones or plan for mulched open areas so you can maneuver among plants.

On the plan and in the garden bed, arrange plants in a triangular or staggered pattern rather than in a line. This gives the most natural appearance as plants grow and spread. It also helps control erosion on slopes by preventing water from running straight downhill.

prepping planting area

Define the new planting area by outlining it on the ground with water-based landscape spray paint, lime, flour, or a garden hose. Next, remove existing weeds and sod, which diminishes the probability of an ongoing weed problem. TOH landscape contractor Roger Cook recommends using a rented sod cutter for clearing large areas, but a spade for working around trees to avoid damaging roots. With the sod gone, loosen the soil with a rotary tiller or shovel. Next, incorporate necessary soil amendments (see page 145).

To get ground covers and perennials off to a good start, spread multi-purpose fertilizer over the planting area. "That saves you from having to fertilize the individual plants," says Cook. Choose a fertilizer that contains 5 to 10 percent of each major nutrient, such as a 5-10-5 or 10-10-10 product, and apply according to the directions. With a rake, work in the fertilizer and level the soil.

When planting numerous small plants over a large area, as in the ground cover planting shown here, spread about 2 inches of mulch

Within each marked boundary, arrange plants to create a flowing tapestry effect.

before planting to avoid harming new plants by burying them in mulch later. (Though if you are preparing just a small garden bed, you can spread mulch between plants after planting.) Shredded bark or aged wood chips make good mulch. These materials stay in place and decompose slowly while discouraging weeds.

putting plants in

Arrange plants in the planting bed while they're still in their containers so that you can tweak the spacing and arrangement. Step back to view the placement, and check it from different viewpoints before proceeding.

Work out from the center of the

Just months after replacing a front lawn with ground cover, the plants have taken hold and started to spread.

planting bed, or from back to front in a bed against a house or fence. Remove plants from their pots one at a time as you're ready to put them in the ground. If mulch is present, pull it away using a three-prong cultivator. Set each plant in the ground with the top of its root ball slightly above the soil level, and cover the roots. Work quickly, pressing down soil to firm around roots, since once you remove a plant from its container, dry air damages the roots.

Right after planting, spread the mulch back over the plants' roots, being careful not to bury their crowns; water thoroughly. If planting on a slope, set each plant into a small, level terrace with a raised ring of soil on the downhill side to prevent water from washing away.

tip: when to till (and when not to) Never till soil when it is too wet, or you will reduce its drainage capacity. To test soil moisture, take a handful of soil and squeeze it. If the soil stays loosely formed or is slightly crumbly when you release your grip, it is perfect for tilling. If it sticks together or oozes water, it is too wet. Wait a day or so and try again. (See page 144 for more on soil types.)

planting trees and large shrubs

The right tree planted in the right spot can last for a lifetime. So be sure to find out the mature size of a tree you are considering and allow for its growth.

Preparing to plant When planting a tree, extend the planting bed at least 2 to 4 feet beyond the trunk. This allows room to mow around the tree without cutting too close to the trunk and possibly damaging it. Provide a low-branching tree a planting area large enough to encompass the diameter of the branches at maturity. Otherwise you'll have to duck to mow. Mulching the open area around the tree cuts down on maintenance and makes it appear more a part of the overall landscape.

When you are ready to plant, remove weeds and sod over the entire planting site, and till or spade to loosen the soil.

Digging the hole Following Roger Cook's method, make the hole three to four times the width of the root ball and slant the sides outward slightly. Roger makes the hole 2 to 3 inches shallower than the height of the root ball, so once the tree is planted, the top of the root ball is slightly above the soil level. Measure the root ball from the bottom of the

container or ball to the trunk flare (where the trunk widens at the soil and merges with the roots). With a balled-and-burlapped tree, if the flare is not visible, untie the twine and remove some of the burlap to locate the flare, but disturb the root ball as little as possible.

Make the planting hole three to four times the width of the root ball and 2 to 3 inches shallower. Dig into the sides of the hole to make it wider at the top than at the base.

Planting a container tree

Remove the tree from its container and brush the soil off the outer few inches of the root ball. Tease or pry apart matted roots and spread them horizontally to encourage them to grow outward. Cut off circling roots where they originate.

Next, place the tree in the hole so the trunk flare is just above the soil level. If necessary, readjust the depth of the planting hole. Partially backfill the hole and water thoroughly to eliminate air pockets that could cause the roots to dry out.

Most new trees need little in the way of fertilizer or amendments at planting time, unless a soil test indicates they are necessary. Roger routinely adds a very mild 3-4-3 fertilizer that includes beneficial

Use your shovel handle (or any convenient straightedge) to check soil level and adjust the plant's height. Where soil is heavy clay, leave it 3 inches higher than surrounding grade, 2 inches above grade otherwise.

Once plant height is set, begin backfilling with excavated soil. Water thoroughly when half the backfill is in place to settle soil and eliminate air pockets.

Complete backfilling, then fashion a water-holding basin around the edge of the planting hole. Mulch, but take care to keep the material away from the base of the trunk.

fungi (mycorrhiza) to the backfill mix and has good results.

Thoroughly water the root ball and soil in the partially filled hole and then finish backfilling. Finally, build a ring of soil several inches high around the edge of the planting hole to create a watering basin and fill it with water.

Ideally the trunk of your new tree will be strong enough to stand upright after planting. Routinely staking trees is not recommended, because trees that are allowed to sway naturally grow stronger and faster than those staked at planting time. If you plant in a very windy site, however, staking will support the tree until the roots become established, but remove the stake as soon as practical and check annually to make sure the ties aren't too tight.

Planting a balled-and-burlapped tree After determining the proper hole depth, set the tree in the hole, supporting the bottom of the root ball as you work. Don't lift the tree by the trunk or drop it into place. Backfill around the bottom third of the ball. Next, remove pinning nails and use wire cutters and scissors to cut away and discard all visible wire, string, and burlap. Any material that remains at the bottom of the root ball should not inhibit the establishment or the growth of the tree, Roger says. Finally, follow the backfilling and watering steps described above.

After planting Remove any nursery tags from the branches to prevent girdling as the tree grows. Spread mulch 2 to 3 inches deep over the planting site, but don't let it touch the trunk; that could encourage disease.

Water newly planted trees regularly and deeply so water soaks past the tree's roots. If you're not sure how deep water is penetrating, check the depth with a screwdriver or trowel. Even drought-tolerant trees require supplemental water for at least the first two years.

tip: buying a new tree

Trees are expensive, so shop around to find one of good quality. Make sure its branches are evenly spaced in all directions. Choose one with a trunk that is rigid and able to stand on its own without staking. If you're looking for a multi-trunked tree, choose one with branches that diverge close to the soil level. Leaves should have a healthy, even color and be free of pests. Reject trees with wounds or nicks in the bark; they can serve as entry points for pests or disease. Check the root system. It should feel moist, and you should see thin, light-colored fibrous roots. Circling or kinked roots at or above the soil level can girdle the trunk as the tree grows.

On a balled-and-burlapped tree, the covering should be intact and the roots concealed. The root ball should feel firm (uncracked) and moist.

Before leaving the nursery, ask for a copy of the plant warranty and save it with your sales receipt.

choosing and using plants

This section will help you choose plants to suit different parts of your landscape. Under each group of plants—trees, shrubs, vines, ground covers, and perennials—you'll find lists of plants suitable for specific uses. Common names are given followed by their botanical counterparts. Both are important, since common names can vary from one region to another, while scientific names are nearly universal. For some plants, cultivated varieties (cultivars) are often the most desirable form, and the lists provide those names in single quotation marks.

Hardiness Following the common and scientific names is the average minimum low temperature the plant is known to tolerate, in degrees Fahrenheit. Like all attempts to rate plant hardiness, these temperatures are a guide and are not definitive. Low temperature is the most common factor that limits where a plant will grow, but it's not the only one. Other factors, such as high summer temperatures, soil fertility and moisture, snow cover (or lack of it), humidity, and exposure to sun and wind also figure prominently in a plant's ability to adapt.

With large trees or shrubs, protect your investment by playing it safe. These are long-lived plants, and you

Fragrant flowers of a deciduous saucer magnolia bloom from late winter into spring, both before leaves emerge and as they open.

want them to survive whatever extremes they'll encounter over many years. Take a chance, however, on plants that are smaller, don't normally live many years, and are less expensive.

Exposure Sunlight, or the lack of it, is another important factor to consider when you are choosing plants. Full sun means 6 or more hours of direct sunshine per day; less than that and you are dealing with part sun/ shade (3 to 6 hours of sun) to full shade (less than 3 hours of sun). Observe your garden's sun and shade patterns and then place plants where they will get the amount of light they

need for optimal growth; otherwise they will perform poorly.

Invasive plants As you choose plants for your garden, avoid those known to be invasive. These plants are likely to escape the boundaries of your garden and overwhelm local native plants. Norway maple and purple loosestrife are well-known examples, but often it's not black or white: a plant may be a noxious weed in one situation or region but not in another. Before landscaping, ask your local cooperative extension office or native plant organization about invasive plants.

trees

Before planting a tree, know its ultimate size and plant it only if there's plenty of space. That's the only way to keep growth from encroaching on buildings, other trees, or power lines. Some trees, such as birch, cherry, and flowering crabapple, are relatively short lived, while others, such as gingko, London plane tree, and oaks, can live hundreds of years and attain impressive size. If you want trees to screen a view, think long term and use long-lived ones.

TREES WITH STRIKING FLOWERS

Flowering trees are the stars of any landscape. Plant one where it will be easily appreciated, and choose a kind that will complement your home's architecture as well as the overall color scheme of your house and landscape.

- Red horsechestnut,
  Aesculus carnea 'Briotii'; –30°
- Hong Kong orchid tree,
  Bauhinia blakeana; 30°
- Common catalpa,
  Catalpa bignonioides; –20°
- Desert willow,
  Chilopsis linearis; 10°
- Fringe tree,
  Chionanthus virginicus; –20°
- Flowering dogwood,
  Cornus florida; –20°
- Kousa dogwood,
  Cornus kousa; –15°
- Jacaranda,
  Jacaranda mimosifolia; 30°

- Crape myrtle,
  Lagerstroemia indica
  'Choctaw', 'Natchez',
  'Wichita'; 0°
- Southern magnolia,
  Magnolia grandiflora; 0°
- Saucer magnolia,
  Magnolia soulangeana; –20°
- Flowering crabapple, *Malus*
  'Donald Wyman', 'Harvest
  Gold', 'Prairifire'; –30°

- Japanese flowering cherry,
  Prunus serrulata; –10°
- Higan cherry, *Prunus subhirtella*; –10°
- Yoshino flowering cherry, *Prunus
  yedoensis*; –10°

TREES FOR PATIOS

Choose among the following trees for patios and terraces. Their mature size—about 20 feet tall—means they fit spaces that many trees rapidly outgrow. Equally important, these are neat, "well-behaved" trees that produce minimal litter.

- Trident maple,
  Acer buergeranum; –20°
- Paperbark maple,
  Acer griseum; –30°

ABOVE: Crape myrtles are choice trees for hot summer regions. LEFT: From late fall to spring, gardeners in mild climates can enjoy the exotic 6-inch-wide blossoms of the Hong Kong orchid tree.

- Japanese maple,
  Acer palmatum; –10°
- Apple serviceberry,
  Amelanchier grandiflora; –20°
- Gold medallion tree,
  Cassia leptophylla; 25°
- Littleleaf palo verde,
  Cercidium microphyllum; 15°
- Palo brea, *Cercidium praecox*; 20°
- Eastern redbud,
  Cercis canadensis; –20°
- Chinese fringe tree,
  Chionanthus retusus; –10°
- Cornelian cherry, *Cornus mas*; –20°
- Australian willow,
  Geijera parviflora; 20°
- Thornless honey locust,
  Gleditsia triacanthos inermis; –30°
- Two-winged silver bell,
  Halesia diptera; –20°
- Crape myrtle, *Lagerstroemia indica*
  'Choctaw', 'Natchez', 'Wichita'; 0°
- Australian tea tree,
  Leptospermum laevigatum; 25°
- Sweet michelia,
  Michelia doltsopa; 25°
- Tall stewartia,
  Stewartia monadelpha; –10°

Abundant blooms of 'Snowdrift' flowering crabapple are followed by orange-red fruit. This disease-resistant tree has a rounded form.

SMALL TREES

Trees that grow to about 20 feet tall may not be majestic but can still have a big impact. If you're planting under or near power lines, they're essential. Plant a row of flowering crabapples to define a boundary or alongside a walkway for a dramatic display of spring flowers and fall fruit. In hot-summer areas, crape myrtle's mottled, exfoliating bark attracts attention even after flowers fade. Plant Young's weeping birch and 'Snow Fountains' Japanese flowering cherry where their weeping branches will stand out. Give 'Winter King' hawthorn and 'Mt. Fuji' Japanese flowering cherry room to extend their spreading branches. Goldenchain tree's 10- to 20-inch-long flower clusters are followed by poisonous pods, making it an undesirable choice if you have young children or curious pets.

- Trident maple, *Acer buergeranum;* –20°
- Japanese maple, *Acer palmatum* 'Bloodgood'; –10°
- Amur maple, *Acer tataricum ginnala* 'Flame'; –40°
- Apple serviceberry, *Amelanchier grandiflora* 'Autumn Brilliance'; –20°
- Young's weeping birch, *Betula pendula* 'Youngii'; –40°
- Western redbud, *Cercis occidentalis;* 0°
- Hinoki false cypress, *Chamaecyparis obtusa* 'Gracilis'; –30°
- Chinese fringe tree, *Chionanthus retusus;* –10°
- Fringe tree, *Chionanthus virginicus;* –20°
- Green hawthorn, *Crataegus viridis* 'Winter King'; –20°
- Yaupon, *Ilex vomitoria;* 10°
- Goldenchain tree, *Laburnum watereri;* 0°
- Crape myrtle, *Lagerstroemia* 'Apalachee', 'Osage', 'Sioux'; 0°
- Star magnolia, *Magnolia stellata;* –20°
- Flowering crabapple, *Malus* 'Adirondack', 'Snowdrift', 'Prairifire'; –30°
- Japanese flowering cherry, *Prunus serrulata* 'Mt. Fuji', 'Snow Fountains'; –10°

TREES FOR FALL FOLIAGE COLOR

Throughout much of North America, the natural landscape becomes a blaze of fiery colors in fall. These trees offer reliable foliage displays in gardens. Fullmoon maple and larch appreciate some shade, while others, such as maidenhair tree and Yoshino flowering cherry, demand full sun.

- Vine maple, *Acer circinatum;* 10°
- Fullmoon maple, *Acer japonicum* 'Vitifolium'; –20°
- Japanese maple, *Acer palmatum;* –10°
- Scarlet maple, *Acer rubrum;* –40°
- Sugar maple, *Acer saccharum;* –30°
- Apple serviceberry, *Amelanchier grandiflora* 'Autumn Brilliance'; –20°
- Flowering dogwood, *Cornus florida;* –20°

Japanese persimmon has tasty fruit and exceptional ornamental qualities. It is a good small shade tree, reaching 30 or more feet tall.

- American smoke tree,
  Cotinus obovatus; –30°
- Green hawthorn,
  Crataegus viridis 'Winter King'; –20°
- Japanese persimmon,
  Diospyros kaki; 0°
- Maidenhair tree, *Ginkgo biloba*; –20°
- Crape myrtle, *Lagerstroemia indica*
  'Choctaw', 'Natchez', 'Wichita'; 0°
- European larch, *Larix decidua*; –40°
- Western larch, *Larix occidentalis*; –30°
- American sweet gum,
  Liquidambar styraciflua; –10°
- Sour gum, *Nyssa sylvatica*; –20°
- Sourwood,
  Oxydendrum arboreum; –25°

Red maple, native to low, wet areas of eastern North America, grows to 60 feet tall by 40 feet wide, sometimes larger.

- Chinese pistache,
  Pistacia chinensis; 0°
- Yoshino flowering cherry,
  Prunus yedoensis; –10°
- Golden larch,
  Pseudolarix amabilis; –20°

TREES FOR SOGGY SOIL

Poorly drained areas or low spots always pose a challenge. Trees that have evolved in moist areas—flood plains, stream sides, or swamps—are well suited to damp sites, because their roots can cope with limited access to oxygen. Bald cypress can actually grow in standing water. Scarlet maple, black alder, and weeping willow can take

Weeping willow, a fast-growing tree 30 to 50 feet tall and wide, thrives when planted near water or in moist soil.

seasonal flooding. In most cases, the trees are deciduous. Many, such as London plane tree, swamp white oak, and sour gum, can reach massive proportions.

- Scarlet maple, *Acer rubrum*; –40°
- Black alder, *Alnus glutinosa*; –30°
- River birch,
  Betula nigra 'Heritage'; –30°
- American sweet gum,
  Liquidambar styraciflua; –10°
- Dawn redwood, *Metasequoia glyptostroboides*; –15°
- Sour gum, *Nyssa sylvatica*; –20°
- London plane tree,
  Platanus acerifolia; –20°
- Swamp white oak,
  Quercus bicolor; –30°
- Weeping willow, *Salix babylonica*; –10°
- Bald cypress, *Taxodium distichum*; –20°

Plum-colored spring leaves of Japanese maples complement the deep rose blossoms of 'Cherokee Chief' flowering dogwood, towering above.

■ Western hackberry,
   Celtis reticulata; –20°
■ Eastern redbud,
   Cercis canadensis; –20°
■ Western redbud,
   Cercis occidentalis; 0°
■ Chitalpa, *Chitalpa tashkentensis;* –10°
■ Texas olive, *Cordia boissieri;* 30°
■ Pagoda dogwood,
   Cornus alternifolia; –30°
■ Giant dogwood,
   Cornus controversa; –10°
■ Flowering dogwood,
   Cornus florida; –20°
■ Green hawthorn,
   Crataegus viridis 'Winter King'; –20°
■ Thornless honey locust,
   Gleditsia triacanthos inermis; –30°
■ Silver bell, *Halesia carolina;* –20°
■ Crape myrtle, *Lagerstroemia indica*
   'Choctaw', 'Natchez', 'Wichita'; 0°
■ Olive, *Olea europaea* (choose
   a fruitless variety); 10°
■ Chinese pistache,
   Pistacia chinensis; 0°
■ Japanese pagoda tree,
   Sophora japonica; –20°
■ Japanese snowdrop tree,
   Styrax japonicus; –10°
■ Japanese zelkova,
   Zelkova serrata; –15°

Paperbark maple sheds its old bark to reveal patches of smooth new bark. The tree eventually reaches 25 feet high.

TREES TO GARDEN UNDER

When designing a garden, use multiple layers of plants to create a dynamic landscape. Flower beds of annuals and perennials or sweeps of ground covers visually link up with trees. Trees with deep root systems, such as western hackberry and Japanese zelkova, allow other plants nearby to compete for nutrition and moisture. Others, such as pearl acacia and redbud, have spreading, somewhat open canopies that let in light to support plant growth below.

■ Pearl acacia, *Acacia podalyriifolia;* 20°
■ River birch, *Betula nigra* 'Heritage';
   –30°
■ Paper birch, *Betula papyrifera;* –50°
■ Common hackberry,
   Celtis occidentalis; –40°

TREES WITH PROMINENT BARK

Interesting foliage and striking flowers are reasons enough to grow trees, but some trees have such unusual bark that this feature alone makes them worth including in your landscape. Some bark is multicolored, as in ghost gum, lacebark pine, and Korean stewartia. Other bark is blocky like alligator skin, as in American persimmon, or smooth like metal, as in common manzanita. Paperbark maple and river birch have peeling, flaking bark that sheds attractively as their trunks grow. Place these interesting trees in key positions in the landscape where you can enjoy their striking bark, particularly in winter.

■ Paperbark maple, *Acer griseum;* –30°
■ Coral bark maple, *Acer palmatum*
   'Sango Kaku'; –10°
■ Striped maple, *Acer*
   pensylvanicum; –40°
■ Madrone, *Arbutus menziesii;* 0°
■ Common manzanita,
   Arctostaphylos manzanita; 25°
■ Himalayan birch,
   Betula jacquemontii; –20°

- River birch,
  Betula nigra 'Heritage'; −30°
- Paper birch, *Betula papyrifera*; −50°
- Incense cedar,
  Calocedrus decurrens; −20°
- American persimmon,
  Diospyros virginiana; −30°
- Ghost gum,
  Eucalyptus pauciflora; 20°
- American beech,
  Fagus grandifolia; −30°
- European beech,
  Fagus sylvatica, −20°
- Japanese crape myrtle,
  Lagerstroemia fauriei; −10°
- Lacebark pine, *Pinus bungeana*; −30°
- Birch bark cherry, *Prunus serrula*; −10°
- Korean stewartia,
  Stewartia koreana; −20°
- Water gum, *Tristaniopsis laurina*; 25°
- Chinese elm, *Ulmus parvifolia*; −20°

Horizontal branches of Japanese snow-drop tree spread as wide as or wider than the tree is tall. Mature height is 30 feet.

Handsome peeling reddish-brown bark is the outstanding feature of evergreen madrones, native to the Pacific Coast Range.

SHADE-TOLERANT TREES

Established landscapes often contain a few mature trees whose canopies cast varying amounts of shade onto the ground. By using trees that originate in the forest, you can replicate an understory that tolerates shady conditions. Maples in their native habitat often grow among forest trees, as do Korean stewartia and Japanese snowdrop trees. These trees appreciate even moisture throughout the year, and many have colorful fall leaves. Beneficial conditions are found on the north side of buildings, where these trees, shielded from the strong midday sun, do well.

- David's maple, *Acer davidii*; −20°
- Fullmoon maple, *Acer japonicum*; −20°
- Japanese maple, *Acer palmatum*; −10°
- Downy serviceberry,
  Amelanchier arborea; −30°
- Apple serviceberry,
  Amelanchier grandiflora; −20°
- Pawpaw tree, *Asimina triloba*; −10°
- Eastern redbud,
  Cercis canadensis; −20°
- Pagoda dogwood,
  Cornus alternifolia; −30°
- Flowering dogwood,
  Cornus florida; −20°
- Oyama magnolia,
  Magnolia sieboldii; −10°
- American hop hornbeam,
  Ostrya virginiana; −20°
- Persian parrotia, *Parrotia persica*; −30°
- Yew pine,
  Podocarpus macrophyllus; 10°
- Korean stewartia,
  Stewartia koreana; −20°
- Japanese snowdrop tree,
  Styrax japonicus; −10°
- Canada hemlock,
  Tsuga canadensis; −30°

shrubs

Shrubs are the hard-working plants of any landscape. They form hedges, barriers, and screens that define garden spaces. They anchor slopes and serve as ground covers. Winter silhouettes of long-lived shrubs add structure and graceful lines to the garden. Fruiting shrubs attract and nourish birds.

Foliage alone makes shrubs such as Japanese aucuba, boxwoods, box honeysuckles, and yews stand out. Others, such as rhododendrons, are available in every flower color except black. In size, rhodies have an amazing range, from low mounds to 30-foot trees. Oleander and common lilac, on the other hand, offer much less choice.

Because of their woody growth, shrubs need occasional pruning to clear away dead wood and to improve flowering. On some long-lived shrubs, such as lilacs, periodically remove the oldest stems all the way to the ground. This allows new shoots to fill their space. Shrubs used as formal hedges need the most frequent maintenance to keep them in best form, often requiring shearing two or more times a year.

SHRUBS WITH STRIKING FLOWERS

Eye-catching flowering shrubs have a place in every home landscape. They give structure to plantings while providing bursts of color at varying times of year: camellias from late fall into spring, rhododendrons in spring and early summer, roses from summer to late-autumn frosts. With good planning, you can have a shrub blooming in your landscape every month of the growing season. As a bonus, include some fragrant plants, such as gardenias, sweet mock orange, roses, and lilacs. Also include some shrubs that attract fauna: butterfly bush and crape myrtle draw butterflies; lemon bottle

In midsummer, 6- to 12-inch-long flower clusters of butterfly bush that are irresistible to butterflies appear on the ends of branches.

brush and hibiscus attract hummingbirds. But make sure to plant your shrubs where they will thrive. While many require full sun for best bloom, camellias, hydrangeas, and rhododendrons need some shade to grow well.

- Butterfly bush, *Buddleia davidii* varieties; –10°
- Lemon bottlebrush, *Callistemon citrinus*; 30°
- Japanese camellia, *Camellia japonica* hybrids; 5°
- Sasanqua camellia, *Camellia sasanqua* hybrids; 5°
- Fuzzy deutzia, *Deutzia scabra* varieties; –10°
- Gardenia, *Gardenia jasminoides*; 10°
- Chinese hibiscus, *Hibiscus rosa-sinensis* varieties; 25°
- Smooth hydrangea, *Hydrangea arborescens*; –30°
- Bigleaf hydrangea, *Hydrangea macrophylla* varieties; –10°
- Crape myrtle, *Lagerstroemia* hybrids; 0°
- New Zealand tea tree, *Leptospermum scoparium*; 20°
- Violet silverleaf, *Leucophyllum candidum*; 10°
- Texas ranger, *Leucophyllum frutescens*; 10°
- Oleander, *Nerium oleander*; 15°
- Sweet mock orange, *Philadelphus coronarius*; –20°
- Rhododendron, *Rhododendron* 'Chionoides'; –10°
- Rhododendron, *Rhododendron* 'Fragrantissimum'; 20°
- Rhododendron, *Rhododendron* 'PJM'; –30°
- Royal azalea, *Rhododendron schlippenbachii*; –20°
- Rhododendron, *Rhododendron yakushimanum*; –20°
- Floribunda roses, *Rosa* 'Betty Prior', 'Iceberg', 'Simplicity'; –20°
- Polyantha roses, *Rosa* 'China Doll', 'The Fairy', 'Margo Koster'; –20°
- Harison's yellow rose,

Free-blooming 'Simplicity' roses make a superb informal hedge. They bear 3- to 4-inch clusters of cup-shaped blossoms.

Rosa harisonii; –30°
- Ramanas rose, *Rosa rugosa*; –50°
- Meyer lilac,
  Syringa meyeri 'Palibin'; –30°
- Persian lilac, *Syringa persica*; –30°
- Common lilac, *Syringa vulgaris*; –35°
- Yellow bells, *Tecoma stans*; 25°

SHRUBS WITH SHOW Y FRUIT

Plan your garden for the maximum effect in all four seasons. Firethorn berries add color in late fall; holly berries brighten the glossy foliage during the dark days of winter. Fruit tends to be eye-catching reds, but beautyberries are a lustrous purple, leatherleaf mahonia berries blue, and firethorn can be blazing orange. Migrating and wintering birds feed on chokeberries, winterberries, and many other fruits.

- Strawberry tree,
  Arbutus unedo dwarf varieties; 0°
- Red chokeberry,
  Aronia arbutifolia; –20°
- Black chokeberry,
  Aronia melanocarpa; –30°
- Purple beautyberry,
  Callicarpa dichotoma; –10°

- Japanese beautyberry,
  Callicarpa japonica; –10°
- Cranberry cotoneaster,
  Cotoneaster apiculatus; –20°
- Spreading cotoneaster,
  Cotoneaster divaricatus; –20°
- Rock cotoneaster,
  Cotoneaster horizontalis; –20°
- Willowleaf cotoneaster,
  Cotoneaster salicifolius; –10°
- Strawberry bush,
  Euonymus americanus; –10°
- Spindle tree,
  Euonymus europaea; –20°
- Wilson holly,
  Ilex altaclerensis 'Wilsonii'; 0°
- Holly, *Ilex aquipernyi* 'San Jose',
  'Brilliant'; –10°

Yellow flowers of leatherleaf mahonia appear in early spring, followed by blue berries.

- Winterberry,
  Ilex verticillata 'Winter Red'; –30°
- Himalayan honeysuckle,
  Leycesteria formosa; 20°
- Leatherleaf mahonia,
  Mahonia bealei; 0°
- Bird's-eye bush, *Ochna serrulata*; 25°
- Pomegranate,
  Punica granatum 'Nana'; 10°
- Firethorn, *Pyracantha coccinea*
  'Gnome', 'Kasan', 'Lalandei'; –10°
- Firethorn, *Pyracantha* hybrids
  including 'Mohave', 'Ruby Mound',
  'Teton'; –10°
- Staghorn sumac,
  Rhus typhina 'Laciniata'; –40°
- Golden currant, *Ribes aureum*; –40°
- Sweet box, *Sarcococca ruscifolia*; 10°
- Coral berry,
  Symphoricarpos orbiculatus; –50°
- Red huckleberry,
  Vaccinium parvifolium; –20°
- Viburnum, *Viburnum davidii*; 10°
- European cranberry bush,
  Viburnum opulus; –30°
- Tea viburnum,
  Viburnum setigerum; –20°
- Cranberry bush,
  Viburnum trilobum; –50°

Strawberry tree's urn-shaped flowers and ³/₄-inch fruit appear at the same time. Yellow fruit is young, and red is mature.

FAST-GROWING SHRUBS

Fast-growing shrubs allow even fairly new plantings to look mature and established. Combine any of the following with slower-growing shrubs, which are usually longer lived than their fast-growing counterparts.

- Glossy abelia, *Abelia grandiflora*; –10°
- Butterfly bush,
  Buddleia davidii varieties; –10°
- Blue mist,
  Caryopteris clandonensis; –10°
- Tatarian dogwood, *Cornus alba*; –40°
- Bloodtwig dogwood,
  Cornus sanguinea; –20°
- Redtwig dogwood,
  Cornus stolonifera (C. sericea); –50°
- Bearberry cotoneaster,
  Cotoneaster dammeri; –10°
- Hop bush,
  Dodonaea viscosa; 20°
- Border forsythia,
  Forsythia intermedia; –10°
- Broadleaf,
  Griselinia littoralis; 10°

In late winter and early spring, yellow blossoms blanket forsythia's branches. Medium-sized rounded green leaves follow.

- Rose of Sharon,
  Hibiscus syriacus; –15°
- Peegee hydrangea,
  Hydrangea paniculata; –30°
- Sweet mock orange,
  Philadelphus coronarius; –20°
- English laurel,
  Prunus laurocerasus; –10°
- French pussy willow,
  Salix caprea; –10°
- Pussy willow,
  Salix discolor; –30°
- Rose-gold pussy willow,
  Salix gracilistyla; –20°
- Dappled willow,
  Salix integra 'Hakuro Nishiki'; –20°

SHRUBS FOR DRY SITES

Baking-hot slopes, steep banks where rain drains away, and sandy soils present challenges to gardeners. Yet even these extremely dry sites can support interesting shrubs if you're careful about selecting adaptable plants. Even low-water-use plants, however, require supplemental water through the first year or two, until they become established.

- Strawberry tree, *Arbutus unedo* dwarf varieties; 10°
- Butterfly bush,
  Buddleia davidii varieties; –10°
- Lemon bottlebrush,
  Callistemon citrinus; 30°
- Blue mist,
  Caryopteris clandonensis; –10°
- Wild lilac, *Ceanothus* 'Concha'; 15°

- Smoke tree, *Cotinus coggygria*; –20°
- Five-leaf aralia,
  Eleutherococcus sieboldianus; –20°
- Common flannel bush,
  Fremontodendron californicum; 10°
- Lavender grevillea,
  Grevillea lavandulacea 'Penola'; 20°
- Rosemary grevillea,
  Grevillea rosmarinifolia; 20°
- Shrub verbena, *Lantana camara*; 20°
- English lavender,
  Lavandula angustifolia; –20°
- Lavandin, *Lavandula intermedia*; –10°
- Spanish lavender,
  Lavandula stoechas; 10°
- New Zealand tea tree,
  Leptospermum scoparium; 20°
- Oleander, *Nerium oleander*; 15°
- Common ninebark,
  Physocarpus opulifolius; –40°
- Tobira, *Pittosporum tobira*; 20°
- Firethorn, *Pyracantha coccinea*; –10°
- Shining sumac, *Rhus copallina*; –20°

English lavender has fragrant deep-purple flowers and medium-sized green leaves on plants 1½ to 2 feet tall.

- Desert sumac, *Rhus microphylla;* 0°
- Ramanas rose, *Rosa rugosa;* –50°
- Rosemary,
  Rosmarinus officinalis; 10°
- Cleveland sage,
  Salvia clevelandii; 10°
- Double bridal wreath, *Spiraea cantoniensis* 'Flore Pleno'; –10°
- Adam's needle,
  Yucca filamentosa; –20°

SHRUBS FOR SHADE

Shade-loving shrubs originated under forest canopies and along woodland edges, and for this reason they thrive in minimal sunshine. Elegant leaves seem to be a product of this background, and flowers often are produced in prodigious quantities, as in camellia, fuchsia, and rhododendron. Because of their forest origins, many need soil that is evenly moist.

- Japanese aucuba,
  Aucuba japonica; 5°
- Korean boxwood,
  Buxus microphylla koreana; –20°
- True dwarf boxwood, *Buxus sempervirens* 'Suffruticosa'; –10°
- Japanese camellia,
  Camellia japonica hybrids; 5°
- Sasanqua camellia,
  Camellia sasanqua hybrids; 5°
- Summersweet, *Clethra alnifolia;* –30°
- Dwarf fothergilla,
  Fothergilla gardenii; –20°
- Fothergilla, *Fothergilla major;* –20°
- Fuchsia, *Fuchsia boliviana;* 35°
- Fuchsia, *Fuchsia magellanica;* 0°
- Salal, *Gaultheria shallon;* –10°
- Witch hazel,
  Hamamelis intermedia varieties; –20°
- Sweetspire, *Itea virginica;* –10°

- Mountain laurel,
  Kalmia latifolia; –20°
- Delavay osmanthus,
  Osmanthus delavayi; 0°
- Holly-leaf osmanthus, *Osmanthus heterophyllus* 'Gulftide'; 0°
- Rhododendron,
  Rhododendron 'Fragrantissima'; 20°
- Rhododendron,
  Rhododendron 'PJM'; –30°
- Rhododendron,
  Rhododendron yakushimanum; –20°
- Sweet box,
  Sarcococca hookerana humilis; –10°
- Japanese yew,
  Taxus cuspidata 'Nana'; –20°
- Yew, *Taxus media* 'Hicksii'; –20°
- Viburnum, *Viburnum davidii;* 10°
- Arrowwood,
  Viburnum dentatum; –40°

SHRUBS FOR AUTUMN COLOR

In climates where low fall temperatures trigger a chemical reaction that turns the leaves of deciduous plants brilliant gold, red, and orange, you can enhance your yard with plants that display colorful fall foliage. Place these shrubs where you can enjoy them near walkways, decks, and patios, or where you can view them from indoors.

All the plants on this list develop colorful leaves in fall. A few also offer handsome fall fruit; these are noted after the botanical name.

- Apple serviceberry, *Amelanchier grandiflora* 'Autumn Brilliance'; –20°
- Allegheny serviceberry,
  Amelanchier laevis; –20°

Deeply lobed leaves of oakleaf hydrangea turn deep red and purple in fall; here they contrast with grasses and a smoke tree.

- Summersweet, *Clethra alnifolia;* –30°
- Cranberry cotoneaster,
  Cotoneaster apiculatus, fruit; –20°
- Spreading cotoneaster,
  Cotoneaster divaricatus, fruit; –20°
- Rock cotoneaster,
  Cotoneaster horizontalis, fruit; –20°
- Dwarf fothergilla,
  Fothergilla gardenii; –20°
- Fothergilla, *Fothergilla major;* –20°
- Witch hazel,
  Hamamelis intermedia varieties; –20°
- Oakleaf hydrangea,
  Hydrangea quercifolia; –20°
- Heavenly bamboo, *Nandina domestica* 'Harbour Dwarf'; 0°
- Pomegranate,
  Punica granatum, fruit; 10°
- Pontic azalea,
  Rhododendron luteum; –20°
- Fragrant sumac,
  Rhus aromatica, fruit; –30°
- Shining sumac, *Rhus copallina;* –20°
- Staghorn sumac,
  Rhus typhina 'Laciniata', fruit; –40°
- Bridal wreath spiraea,
  Spiraea prunifolia 'Plena'; –20°
- Arrowwood, *Viburnum dentatum;* –40°
- Linden viburnum,
  Viburnum dilatatum, fruit; –20°

SHRUBS FOR SHEARED HEDGES

The following two lists include plants that can be pruned or sheared into formal hedges to serve as walls around a garden room, as a property divider, or as a low boundary for a terrace or patio. Be sure to match the ultimate size of the plant to the height of your intended hedge.

Maintaining a sheared hedge requires labor-intensive pruning—sometimes several times a year—to keep edges neat. When you prune, shape the hedge so that the base is wider than the top, so that all leaves receive sun and stay healthy. Allow enough room around the hedge for maintaining it; in many cases, you will need to set a ladder next to it for pruning. In cold-winter climates, keep in mind where plows will push snow, and avoid placing shrubs too close to roads and driveways. Road salt also can damage nearby hedge plants.

SHEARED HEDGES TO 3 FEET

- Japanese boxwood, *Buxus microphylla japonica;* –10°
- Korean boxwood, *Buxus microphylla koreana;* –20°
- True dwarf boxwood, *Buxus sempervirens* 'Suffruticosa'; –10°
- Natal plum, *Carissa macrocarpa;* 20°
- Inkberry, *Ilex glabra* 'Shamrock'; –20°
- Yaupon, *Ilex vomitoria* 'Nana'; 10°
- African boxwood, *Myrsine africana;* 20°
- Alpine currant, *Ribes alpinum* 'Green Mound'; –50°
- Japanese yew, *Taxus cuspidata* 'Nana'; –20°
- Evergreen huckleberry, *Vaccinium ovatum;* 0°

SHEARED HEDGES TO 8 FEET

- Glossy abelia, *Abelia grandiflora;* –10°
- English boxwood, *Buxus sempervirens;* –10°
- Chinese holly, *Ilex cornuta* 'Berries Jubilee'; 0°

Versatile yew pines can be grown as shrubs or trees, clipped or not. In this formal garden, they are sheared to line a walkway.

- Japanese holly, *Ilex crenata;* –5°
- Texas ranger, *Leucophyllum frutescens;* 10°
- Japanese privet, *Ligustrum japonicum* 'Rotundifolium'; 10°
- Box honeysuckle, *Lonicera nitida;* –10°
- True myrtle, *Myrtus communis;* 15°
- Yew pine, *Podocarpus macrophyllus;* 10°
- Yew, *Taxus media* 'Hatfieldii', 'Hicksii'; –20°
- Bush germander, *Teucrium fruticans;* 10°

Ribbons of clipped boxwood hedge make a bold statement as they define a mulched path and lend structure to the landscape.

NATURAL HEDGES TO 8 FEET

A looser, more natural-looking hedge suits an informal landscape. Like a sheared hedge, the natural hedge can serve as a divider between different parts of the garden, as a privacy screen, or as a seasonal focal point. Evergreen hedges, such as grevillea, holly, and osmanthus, can provide year-round screening in warm regions. A hedge of flowering quince or spiraea will put on a dramatic floral display in spring; holly and winterberry hold their bold displays of bright red or orange fruits all winter, providing a magnet for birds. Natural hedges require much less work than sheared hedges, but you still need to routinely remove dead branches and unwanted growth.

A good candidate for an informal hedge, oleander grows moderately fast and blooms from spring to fall.

- Japanese aucuba,
  Aucuba japonica; 5°
- Flowering quince, *Chaenomeles* 'Apple Blossom', 'Coral Sea', 'Nivalis', 'Red Ruffles'; –20°
- Grevillea,
  Grevillea 'Canberra Gem'; 20°
- Rosemary grevillea,
  Grevillea rosmarinifolia; 20°
- Holly, *Ilex* 'September Gem'; –10°
- Winterberry,
  Ilex verticillata 'Winter Red'; –30°
- Oleander, *Nerium oleander* intermediate-sized varieties; 15°
- Delavay osmanthus,
  Osmanthus delavayi; 0°
- Holly-leaf osmanthus, *Osmanthus heterophyllus* 'Gulftide'; 0°
- Common ninebark, *Physocarpus opulifolius* 'Diablo', 'Luteus'; –40°
- English laurel, *Prunus laurocerasus* 'Schipkaensis', 'Zabeliana'; –10°
- Double bridal wreath, *Spiraea cantoniensis* 'Flore Pleno'; –10°
- Spiraea, *Spiraea vanhouttei;* –30°
- Viburnum,
  Viburnum 'Chesapeake'; –10°
- Viburnum, *Viburnum rhytidophylloides* 'Allegheny'; –20°
- Weigela, *Weigela* 'Bristol Ruby', 'Newport Red'; –30°

SHRUBS FOR ESPALIERS

Some shrubs make great candidates for training flat against a wall or fence. This technique, much favored in European gardens, is known by its French name, espalier. Shrubs with long stems or droopy, flexible ones are suitable for such treatment. You tie the stems onto a series of wires set parallel to each other and firmly affixed to a flat surface. With careful pruning, you create a pleasing framework of branches. Though the training process is rather exacting, once the framework is established, routine pruning is all that's necessary. While certainly not low maintenance, an espaliered shrub imparts an artistic, sophisticated quality to your garden.

- Wild lilac, *Ceanothus delilianus* 'Gloire de Versailles'; 10°
- Rock cotoneaster,
  Cotoneaster horizontalis; –20°
- Willowleaf cotoneaster,
  Cotoneaster salicifolius; –10°
- Common flannel bush,
  Fremontodendron californicum; 10°
- Southern flannel bush,
  Fremontodendron mexicanum; 20°
- Firethorn, *Pyracantha coccinea* 'Gnome', 'Kasan', 'Lalandei'; –10°
- Firethorn, *Pyracantha* 'Mohave'; –10°

With consistent training and pruning, 'Mohave' pyracantha is easily espaliered in a symmetrical design against a stone wall.

vines

Every landscape can be enhanced by vines—scrambling up a wall, covering a trellis, or weaving through the branches of a tree. Most vines, including bower actinidia and Japanese wisteria, are vigorous growers and will need seasonal pruning to keep them inbounds. Others, such as California Dutchman's pipe and climbing hydrangea, are less vigorous but still need occasional pruning. Many vines are slow to get established, so coddle plants the first season.

Vines climb in a number of ways: with twining stems that wrap clockwise or counterclockwise around supports, as with Carolina jessamine and trumpet honeysuckle; by little tendrils that wrap themselves around supports, like clematis; using suction like disks or aerial roots, as in Boston ivy; or merely growing in a lanky, scrambling way over other plants, like roses.

Always match your vine's growth habit and ultimate size to the structure you intend to grow it on. Large vines weigh an enormous amount and will crush flimsy structures.

FLOWERING VINES

A great many flowering vines are available, and making the right choice can be difficult. Your climate and personal preferences will narrow the field. Place flowering vines in areas of high visibility to add luxuriance to your garden. Their colors can be as

Twining, woody Japanese wisteria displays flower clusters up to 3 feet long on vines reaching three stories tall.

bright and bold as bougainvillea or as soft and muted as star jasmine. Trumpet creepers, among others, attract hummingbirds, and honeysuckles attract butterflies. Quite a few flowering vines feature fragrant blooms, which scent the garden air. Place these vines on arbors and pergolas near paths, doorways, and patios.

- Golden trumpet, *Allamanda cathartica*; 20°
- *Bougainvillea* varieties; 25°
- Chinese trumpet creeper, *Campsis grandiflora*; 0°
- Hybrid trumpet creeper, *Campsis tagliabuana*; –10°
- Evergreen clematis, *Clematis armandii*; 0°
- Anemone clematis, *Clematis montana*; –10°
- Golden clematis, *Clematis tangutica*; –10°
- Sweet autumn clematis, *Clematis terniflora*; –20°
- Carolina jessamine, *Gelsemium sempervirens*; 0°
- Climbing hydrangea, *Hydrangea anomala petiolaris*; –30°
- Common white jasmine, *Jasminum officinale*; 20°
- Jasmine, *Jasminum polyanthum*; 20°
- Scarlet trumpet honeysuckle, *Lonicera brownii* 'Dropmore Scarlet'; –30°
- Goldflame honeysuckle, *Lonicera heckrottii*; –25°
- Giant Burmese honeysuckle, *Lonicera hildebrandiana*; 20°
- Trumpet honeysuckle, *Lonicera sempervirens*; –30°

- Climbing rose, *Rosa* 'Cl. Cécile Drunner', 'Golden Showers', 'Cl. Iceberg', 'New Dawn', 'Sally Holmes', 'White Dawn'; –20°
- Japanese hydrangea vine, *Schizophragma hydrangeoides;* –20°
- Star jasmine, *Trachelospermum jasminoides;* 20°
- Japanese wisteria, *Wisteria floribunda;* –20°

SELF-ATTACHING VINES

While some vines scramble and twine to climb, others have specially adapted plant parts that enable them to affix to structures. Aerial roots and adhesive disks are two such parts that help plants move skyward. Persian ivy has aerial roots along its stems, which form and grip when they come in contact with a surface. Virginia creeper and Boston ivy cling with little disks that adhere to flat surfaces. Be aware of where you place these

A creeping fig attaches itself firmly to a masonry wall with aerial roots. Regular pruning is required to keep it inbounds.

self-attachers; if you remove some of the vine, their holdfasts may be left behind, marring painted surfaces. You may need to cut back all self-attaching vines periodically to keep them inbounds.

- Hybrid trumpet creeper, *Campsis tagliabuana;* –10°
- Creeping fig, *Ficus pumila;* 10°
- Persian ivy, *Hedera colchica;* 10°
- English ivy, *Hedera helix* 'Baltica'; –20°
- Climbing hydrangea, *Hydrangea anomala petiolaris;* –30°
- Virginia creeper, *Parthenocissus quinquefolia;* –30°
- Boston ivy, *Parthenocissus tricuspidata;* –30°
- Japanese hydrangea vine, *Schizophragma hydrangeoides;* –20°

VINES FOR SHADE

While most flowering vines thrive in full sun, others appreciate some shade. In many cases, what these vines lack in floral display they make up for in luscious foliage. Vines such as Dutchman's pipe and creeping fig are grown for their deep green leaves. Climbing hydrangea and Japanese hydrangea vine bloom beautifully even in partial shade. Grow these vines on east- or north-facing walls or fences where they will be spared baking-hot sun all day. Alternatively, plant these vines under a shaded pergola or an arbor placed under the canopy of trees or in the shadow of buildings.

Large heart-shaped leaves and fast growth make the twining Dutchman's pipe popular for screening a shady porch.

- Kolomikta actinidia, *Actinidia kolomikta;* –20°
- California Dutchman's pipe, *Aristolochia californica;* 10°
- Dutchman's pipe, *Aristolochia macrophylla;* –20°
- Creeping fig, *Ficus pumila;* 10°
- Climbing hydrangea, *Hydrangea anomala petiolaris;* –30°
- Goldflame honeysuckle, *Lonicera heckrottii;* –25°
- Trumpet honeysuckle, *Lonicera sempervirens;* –30°
- Boston ivy, *Parthenocissus tricuspidata;* –30°
- Japanese hydrangea vine, *Schizophragma hydrangeoides;* –20°

EVERGREEN VINES

Just as some trees and shrubs keep their leaves year-round, so do some vines. These evergreen plants give coverage no matter the season. Place them in key locations visible from indoors so you can enjoy the greenery when most other plants have dropped their leaves. When these vines are grown at the limits of their hardiness, the cold will burn their leaves. In a severe cold spell, the vines may become deciduous and die back to the ground.

- Golden trumpet, *Allamanda cathartica;* 20°
- *Bougainvillea* varieties; 25°
- Evergreen clematis, *Clematis armandii;* 0°
- Lace vine, *Fallopia baldschuanica;* –20°
- Creeping fig, *Ficus pumila;* 10°
- Carolina jessamine, *Gelsemium sempervirens;* 0°

- Lilac vine, *Hardenbergia violacea;* 20°
- English ivy, *Hedera helix* 'Baltica'; –20°
- Queen's wreath, *Petrea volubilis;* 25°
- Cape honeysuckle, *Tecoma capensis;* 20°
- Star jasmine, *Trachelospermum jasminoides;* 20°

FAST-GROWING VINES

If you want rapid coverage of a garden structure, choose from the vines listed here. Their vigor makes them good candidates for screening in the garden or softening architecture. Crimson glory vine has large, handsome, abundant leaves that provide

In late summer, flowers of robust sweet autumn clematis provide a soft, billowing counterpoint to an iron security fence.

Sweetly perfumed flowers of star jasmine cloak the twining vine in spring. Glossy green leaves remain attractive in all seasons.

excellent coverage. Sweet autumn clematis does not have large leaf mass, but it can grow 15 feet in a season, and it's smothered in scented flowers in fall. Since many of these vines become quite large, be certain to grow them on fences and garden structures that can take the load.

- Bower actinidia, *Actinidia arguta;* –40°
- Coral vine, *Antigonon leptopus;* 20°
- Crossvine, *Bignonia capreolata;* –10°
- *Bougainvillea* varieties; 25°
- Anemone clematis, *Clematis montana;* –10°
- Sweet autumn clematis, *Clematis terniflora;* –20°

- Violet trumpet vine,
  Clytostoma callistegioides; 20°
- Mattress vine,
  Muehlenbeckia complexa; 10°
- Passion vine,
  Passiflora alatocaerulea; 25°
- California wild grape,
  Vitis californica; 15°
- Crimson glory vine,
  Vitis coignetiae; –20°

VINES WITH FALL-INTEREST FRUIT AND/OR FOLIAGE

Virginia creeper and Boston ivy are favored for their scarlet leaves. Both also produce blue-black berries that hang on into winter, making these plants valuable in several seasons. For this reason, people are willing to put up with the plants' less than

Purple-leaf grape is grown for attractive leaves that emerge downy green, mature to deep purple, and turn deeper purple in autumn.

desirable habit of clinging tenaciously to clapboard, mortared stone, and brick. Plant vines with wild and unkempt growth, such as American bittersweet, away from the house or patio, and choose more well-disciplined vines, such as *Vitis*, for screening near sitting areas. The foliage of this type of vine is attractive even before it turns color.

- American bittersweet,
  Celastrus scandens; –40°
- Sweet autumn clematis,
  Clematis terniflora; –20°
- Virginia creeper,
  Parthenocissus quinquefolia; –30°
- Boston ivy,
  Parthenocissus tricuspidata; –30°
- Chinese magnolia vine,
  Schisandra chinensis; –20°
- California wild grape,
  Vitis californica 'Walker's Ridge'; 15°
- Crimson glory vine,
  Vitis coignetiae; –20°
- Purple-leaf grape,
  Vitis vinifera 'Purpurea'; –10°

A wrought-iron fence supports a flamboyant bougainvillea; in peak summer bloom, the vine brightens the courtyard entrance.

Lady's-mantle is a clump-forming ground cover with velvety scalloped leaves and sprays of yellowish-green spring flowers.

ground covers

Ground cover is a catch all plant group that includes a variety of shrubs, vines, and perennials. The quality they have in common is the habit of creeping over and otherwise covering the ground. Many have a season in which they bloom. Most importantly, they have attractive foliage that stands up well for the whole gardening season. Evergreen ground covers such as ivy, manzanita, juniper, and lily turf provide coverage year-round.

Ground covers have many practical uses: stabilizing a bank, filling in gaps between steppingstones, and substituting for lawn. Once established, ground covers are typically low maintenance, and their dense foliage keeps most weeds at bay. (Weeds are the bane of new plantings. Until a cover is established, a thick mulch is the best defense.) Some, such as bishop's hat and sweet box, "travel" by fleshy stems called rhizomes or stolons, mak-

Grown primarily for their luxuriant and varied foliage, plaintain lilies form graceful mounding clumps that expand each year.

ing them well suited for spreading. Others, such as greenstem forsythia, spread simply by crawling stems, which usually root where they touch the soil.

GROUND COVERS FOR SHADE

Many shade-loving ground covers have attractive flowers. Plantain lily blooms in summer, while most others bloom in the springtime before leafing out. All possess distinctive foliage, which contrasts well with other plants. Evergreen types include lily turf and sweet box; consider placing them where you can view them in winter.

- Carpet bugle, *Ajuga reptans;* –40°
- Lady's-mantle, *Alchemilla mollis;* –30°
- Wild ginger, *Asarum canadense;* –40°
- Wild ginger, *Asarum europaeum;* –30°
- Bishop's hat, *Epimedium grandiflorum;* –20°
- Sweet woodruff, *Galium odoratum;* –20°
- Plantain lily, *Hosta* hybrids; –40°
- Big blue lily turf, *Liriope muscari;* –10°
- Creeping lily turf, *Liriope spicata;* –20°
- Heavenly bamboo, *Nandina domestica* 'Harbour Dwarf'; 0°
- Mondo grass, *Ophiopogon japonicus;* 0°
- Japanese spurge, *Pachysandra terminalis* 'Green Sheen'; –30°
- Sweet box, *Sarcococca hookerana humilis;* –10°
- Baby's tears, *Soleirolia soleirolii;* 30°
- Dwarf periwinkle, *Vinca minor;* –30°

GROUND COVERS TO STABILIZE A SLOPE

Once these ground covers become established, their matlike root systems knit with the soil. Place them in staggered rows to keep erosion to a minimum while root networks expand. Pay extra attention to gentle but thorough watering the first season. Maximize the effect of the flowering varieties by placing them on banks facing your house.

- Glossy abelia, *Abelia grandiflora* 'Prostrata'; –10°
- Manzanita, *Arctostaphylos* 'Emerald Carpet'; 15°
- Monterey manzanita, *Arctostaphylos hookeri*; 10°
- Carmel creeper, *Ceanothus griseus horizontalis* 'Yankee Point'; 20°
- Greenstem forsythia, *Forsythia viridissima* 'Bronxensis'; –10°
- Creeping St. Johnswort, *Hypericum calycinum*; –20°
- Creeping juniper, *Juniperus horizontalis* 'Bar Harbor', 'Blue Chip', 'Plumosa', 'Wiltonii'; –40°
- Japanese garden juniper, *Juniperus procumbens*; –20°
- Lantana, *Lantana montevidensis*; 20°
- Creeping mahonia, *Mahonia repens*; –10°
- Fragrant sumac, *Rhus aromatica* 'Low Grow'; –30°
- Rose, *Rosa* 'Flower Carpet', 'Knock Out', 'White Meidiland', and others; –20°
- Cutleaf stephanandra, *Stephanandra incisa* 'Crispa'; –20°
- Coral berry, *Symphoricarpos orbiculatus*; –50°

Ground-hugging junipers are tough plants that will grow in sun in virtually any well-drained soil, in hot or cool climates.

FLOWERING GROUND COVERS

While ground covers are most often cited for their utility, many, such as yarrow and catmint, also have abundant, showy flowers in full-sun locations. Where it's shady, barrenwort is similarly showy. Choose plants whose blossoms will fit your color scheme. Tie colors into flowerbeds or play off paint colors. Some flowering ground covers, such as twinspur, are long blooming, while others, such as mother-of-thyme, give a brief show of color. Butterflies often flock to the bright drifts of twinspur, trailing African daisy, and verbena. Research the needs of your favorites to make sure they will thrive in the conditions that exist in your yard.

- Woolly yarrow, *Achillea tomentosa*; –30°
- Carpet bugle, *Ajuga reptans*; –40°
- Lady's-mantle, *Alchemilla mollis*; –30°
- Snow-in-summer, *Cerastium tomentosum*; –40°
- Twinspur, *Diascia integerrima*; 10°
- Barrenwort, *Epimedium rubrum* 'Pink Queen', 'Snow Queen'; –20°
- Barrenwort, *Epimedium versicolor* 'Sulphureum'; –20°
- Trailing ice plant, *Lampranthus spectabilis*; 10°
- Catmint, *Nepeta faassonii*; –30°
- Nepeta, *Nepeta* 'Six Hills Giant'; –30°
- Trailing African daisy, *Osteospermum fruticosum*; 20°
- Soapwort, *Saponaria ocymoides*; –30°
- Mother-of-thyme, *Thymus serpyllum*; –20°
- Moss verbena, *Verbena pulchella gracilior* (*V. tenuisecta*); 0°
- Verbena, *Verbena rigida*; 10°
- Dwarf periwinkle, *Vinca minor*; –30°

Trailing African daisies spread rapidly by trailing stems that root as they touch the ground. Plants bloom intermittently all year.

DROUGHT-TOLERANT GROUND COVERS

These plants are adapted to seasonal drought conditions. Sun and heat do not faze them, so they can grow in harsh exposures next to walls or driveways or on sunny slopes. Because they prefer free-draining soil and do not like the combination of heat and humidity, they are not well suited to areas where such conditions prevail. While drought tolerant, these plants appreciate a soaking during a severe, prolonged dry spell.

In spring flower, drought-tolerant moss pink provides brilliant color as it drapes over rocks and clings to soil with creeping stems.

Heat- and drought-tolerant sunrose is at home here on a gentle slope, where it will ramble and eventually spread to 3 feet wide.

- Woolly yarrow, *Achillea tomentosa; –30°*
- Carpet bugle, *Ajuga reptans; –40°*
- Bearberry, *Arctostaphylos uva-ursi; –45°*
- Coyote brush, *Baccharis pilularis; 15°*
- *Bougainvillea* varieties; 25°
- Gazania, *Gazania* hybrids; 10°
- Sunrose, *Helianthemum nummularium; –10°*
- Redondo creeper, *Lampranthus filicaulis; 20°*
- Moss pink, *Phlox subulata; –40°*
- Dwarf rosemary, *Rosmarinus officinalis* 'Prostratus'; 10°
- Lavender cotton, *Santolina chamaecyparissus; –10°*
- Stonecrop, *Sedum kamtschaticum; –20°*
- Stonecrop, *Sedum spurium; –30°*
- Lemon thyme, *Thymus citriodorus; –10°*

GROUND COVERS BETWEEN PAVERS

Spreading plants with small leaves and ground-hugging habits are good candidates for planting between steppingstones and pavers or along the edges of paths. Their scrambling tendency softens stone's angular edges. Although small in stature, these plants have strong constitutions, allowing light foot traffic to pass over them. Several of these plants flower, and some are quite showy. Permit plants to become established before allowing people to walk on them, and clip them occasionally to keep them inbounds.

- Pussy toes, *Antennaria dioica; –20°*
- Wall rockcress, *Arabis caucasica; –30°*
- Sandwort, *Arenaria montana; –30°*
- Common thrift, *Armeria maritima; –30°*
- Chamomile, *Chamaemelum nobile; 0°*

- Bunchberry, *Cornus canadensis;* –50°
- Cranberry cotoneaster, *Cotoneaster apiculatus;* –20°
- Bishop's hat, *Epimedium grandiflorum;* –20°
- Heath, *Erica carnea;* –20°
- Checkerberry, *Gaultheria procumbens;* –40°
- Coral bells, *Heuchera* 'Taffs Joy'; –30°
- Creeping mahonia, *Mahonia repens;* –10°
- Partridgeberry, *Mitchella repens;* –30°
- Sedum, *Sedum* 'Vera Jameson'; –30°
- Foamflower, *Tiarella cordifolia;* –40°
- Sweet violet, *Viola odorata;* –10°

- Dichondra, *Dichondra micrantha;* 20°
- Dymondia, *Dymondia margaretae;* 25°
- Crane's bill, *Erodium reichardii;* 10°
- Green carpet, *Herniaria glabra;* 10°
- Mazus, *Mazus reptans;* –10°
- Blue star creeper, *Pratia pedunculata;* –20°
- Irish moss, *Sagina subulata;* 0°
- Woolly thyme, *Thymus pseudolanuginosus;* –20°
- Korean grass, *Zoysia tenuifolia;* 15°

GROUND COVERS WITH FALL-INTEREST FRUIT AND/OR FOLIAGE

These choices not only provide attractive foliage and flowers during spring and summer, but they also contribute russet, red, and yellow foliage in fall.

Bearberry, bunchberry, cranberry cotoneaster, checkerberry, and creeping mahonia have showy berries that attract wildlife. Plant sedum 'Vera Jameson' and foamflower to extend the color in your perennial garden. Bearberry does well in poor, infertile soils. Sweet violet will even display a second flush of fragrant purple flowers in late fall. Mulch plants well to help them settle in and spread.

- Bearberry, *Arctostaphylos uva-ursi;* –50°
- Heartleaf bergenia, *Bergenia cordifolia* 'Bressingham White'; –40°
- Scotch heather, *Calluna vulgaris* 'Blazeaway', 'Robert Chapman'; –20°

Diminutive bunchberry, here with purple fall foliage and shiny red fruit, sports handsome 2-inch-wide white flowers in spring.

perennials

Perennials are nonwoody plants that have a persistent rootstock and live for more than two years. Most die back each winter, but some, such as evergreen candytuft, New Zealand flax, and yucca, are considered evergreen because their leaves are present year-round. Most are chosen for their flowers, but many have noteworthy foliage.

As varied as any group of plants, perennials grow in cool shade or baking sun and offer virtually year-round blossoms in warm climates if you select plants with differing bloom seasons. Use perennials creatively to cascade down walls, to attract wildlife, and to fashion artistic combinations of texture, color, and mass.

Buy perennials anytime during the growing season as container-grown plants, and in spring as dormant bare-root plants through mail-order nurseries. To protect plants in frigid climates, mulch their crowns in winter after the soil freezes with evergreen boughs or weed-free straw. To maintain perennials, cut back spent foliage and flower stems at the end of winter, divide overgrown clumps when necessary, and deadhead (cut away) spent blossoms during the growing season.

Lenten rose starts blooming in late winter. Clump-forming plants self-sow.

EARLY-BLOOMING PERENNIALS

Where winters are cold, snowy, and prolonged, the first flower of the season is heartily welcomed. Harbingers of spring, such as sharp-leafed hepatica and pasque flower, bloom as soon as snows recede and soil begins to warm. In mild climates, bear's-foot hellebore, Christmas rose, and winter iris bloom in winter. Plant these perennials where you'll be sure to see them, near windows or along paths.

- **Wall rockcress, *Arabis caucasica*; –30°**
- **Common aubrieta, *Aubrieta deltoidea*; –30°**
- **Basket-of-gold, *Aurinia saxatilis*; –30°**
- **Wallflower, *Erysimum* 'Bowles Mauve'; –10°**
- **Large Mediterranean spurge, *Euphorbia characias*; –10°**
- **Cushion spurge, *Euphorbia polychroma*; –30°**
- **Corsican hellebore, *Helleborus argutifolius*; –10°**
- **Bear's-foot hellebore, *Helleborus foetidus*; –10°**

- **Christmas rose, *Helleborus niger*; –30°**
- **Lenten rose, *Helleborus orientalis*; –30°**
- **Sharp-leafed hepatica, *Hepatica acutiloba*; –30°**
- **Liverleaf, *Hepatica nobilis*; –20°**
- **Evergreen candytuft, *Iberis sempervirens*; –20°**
- **Winter iris, *Iris unguicularis*; 0°**
- **Forget-me-not, *Myosotis scorpioides*; –20°**
- **Moss pink, *Phlox subulata*; –40°**
- **Juliana primrose, *Primula juliae* hybrids; –20°**
- **Cowslip lungwort, *Pulmonaria angustifolia*; –30°**
- **Bethlehem sage, *Pulmonaria saccharata*; –30°**
- **Pasque flower, *Pulsatilla vulgaris*; –20°**

PERENNIALS FOR SHADE

A few hours of morning or late-afternoon sun is fine for these shade-loving plants, but avoid hot midday sun. Many of these perennials appreciate moisture-retentive soil and a layer of mulch to keep roots cool in summer. Lady's-mantle, fringed bleeding heart, barrenwort, plantain lily, and Jerusalem cowslip have particularly attractive foliage.

- **Garden monkshood, *Aconitum napellus*; –20°**
- **Lady's-mantle, *Alchemilla mollis*; –30°**
- **Japanese anemone, *Anemone hybrida*; –30°**
- **Windflower, *Anemone nemorosa*; –30°**

- Cast-iron plant, *Aspidistra elatior;* 0°
- False spiraea,
  Astilbe arendsii hybrids; –30°
- Fancy-leafed caladium,
  Caladium bicolor; 20°
- Ivory bells,
  Campanula alliariifolia; –40°
- Bellflower,
  Campanula takesimana; –20°
- Fringed bleeding heart,
  Dicentra eximia; –30°
- Common bleeding heart,
  Dicentra spectabilis; –40°
- Bishop's hat,
  Epimedium grandiflorum; –20°
- Bear's-foot hellebore,
  Helleborus foetidus; –10°
- Lenten rose,
  Helleborus orientalis; –30°
- Christmas rose,
  Helleborus niger; –30°
- Plantain lily, *Hosta* hybrids; –40°
- Dead nettle, *Lamium maculatum;* –30°
- Solomon's seal,
  Polygonatum biflorum; –30°
- Primrose, *Primula sieboldii;* –30°
- Jerusalem cowslip,
  Pulmonaria officinalis; –10°

DROUGHT-TOLERANT PERENNIALS

Water-wise landscapes rely primarily on plants adapted to the garden's climate. Often these are native plants, but succulents, such as stonecrop, and fleshy rooted plants, such as lily-of-the-Nile, also adapt to periods of drought. Likewise, both New Zealand flax and yucca have tough swordlike leaves that resist drought, while wormwood and lamb's ears have gray fuzzy hairs that protect leaves from hot sun by reflecting sunlight. Tough as these plants are, many of them, including yarrow, tickseed, Ozark sundrops, and California fuchsia, have showy flowers.

Flowers of shade-tolerant monkshood bloom in spikelike clusters on stems 2 to 5 feet tall. Plants grow best in moist, rich soil.

- Fernleaf yarrow, *Achillea filipendulina* 'Gold Plate'; –40°
- Common yarrow,
  Achillea millefolium cultivars; –40°
- Moonshine yarrow,
  Achillea 'Moonshine'; –30°
- Lily-of-the-Nile,
  Agapanthus africanus; 20°
- Common wormwood,
  Artemisia absinthium; –30°
- Wormwood, *Artemisia* 'Powis Castle'; 0°
- Beach wormwood,
  Artemisia stellerana; –30°
- Tickseed, *Coreopsis lanceolata;* –30°
- Thread-leaf tickseed,
  Coreopsis verticillata; –30°
- Sea holly,
  Eryngium amethystinum; –40°

'Moonshine' yarrow offers a long season of color, with light-yellow blooms above gray-green foliage from May to September.

- Myrtle spurge,
  Euphorbia myrsinites; –20°
- Blanket flower,
  Gaillardia grandiflora; –40°
- Gaura, *Gaura lindheimeri;* –10°
- White evening primrose,
  Oenothera caespitosa; –30°
- Ozark sundrops,
  Oenothera macrocarpa; –20°
- Russian sage,
  Perovskia atriplicifolia; –20°
- Tuberous Jerusalem sage,
  Phlomis tuberosa; –20°
- Mountain flax,
  Phormium cookianum hybrids; 20°
- New Zealand flax,
  Phormium tenax hybrids; 20°
- Stonecrop, *Sedum telephium (Hylotelephium)* 'Bertram Anderson'; –30°
- Stonecrop,
  Sedum spathulifolium; –20°
- Lamb's ears, *Stachys byzantina;* –30°
- Adam's needle,
  Yucca filamentosa; –20°
- California fuchsia, *Zauschneria californica (Epilobium canum canum);* 10°

Verbena bonariensis *blooms late—from summer until frost. Plants grow 3 to 6 feet tall and look best when massed in the garden.*

LATE-SEASON PERENNIALS

These plants grow happily during spring and summer but put on their biggest show late in the season, when lower temperatures and autumn rains often refresh the landscape. They will add brilliant color to your garden when most plants have long since finished blooming.

- Monkshood,
  Aconitum carmichaelii; –40°
- Japanese anemone,
  Anemone hybrida; –30°
- Heath aster, *Aster ericoides;* –20°
- Frikart's aster, *Aster frikartii*
  'Mönch'; –20°
- False spiraea,
  Astilbe chinensis; –30°
- Dwarf plumbago,
  Ceratostigma plumbaginoides; –10°
- Turtlehead, *Chelone lyonii;* –40°
- Florists' chrysanthemum,
  Chrysanthemum morifolium; –10°
- Bugbane,
  Cimicifuga japonica; –30°

- Black snakeroot,
  Cimicifuga racemosa; –40°
- Twinspur,
  Diascia integerrima; 10°
- Maximilian sunflower,
  Helianthus maximilianii; –30°
- Fountain grass, *Pennisetum alopecuroides* 'Hameln';–10°
- Pincushion flower, *Scabiosa* 'Butterfly Blue', 'Pink Mist'; –40°
- Stonecrop, *Sedum telephium (Hylotelephium)* 'Autumn Joy'; –40°
- Stonecrop, *Sedum telephium (Hylotelephium)* 'Vera Jameson'; –30°
- October daphne, *Sedum sieboldii;* –10°
- Verbena, *Verbena bonariensis;* 0°
- California fuchsia, *Zauschneria californica (Epilobium canum canum);* 10°

TALL PERENNIALS

Upright perennials can lend an architectural presence to the landscape. Some, such as common foxglove and royal beard tongue, can grow from a basal clump to a 3- to 4-foot spire in one season. When fully grown, bear's breech and Joe Pye weed reach the proportions of shrubs. You can plant them as backdrops for smaller perennials, mix them among shrubs, or use them singly for a dramatic accent. New Zealand flax, with year-round colorful leaves, is dramatic by itself.

'Sundowner' New Zealand flax, with variegated swordlike evergreen foliage to 6 feet tall, makes a showy garden accent.

- Bear's breech,
  Acanthus balcanicus; 0°
- Bear's breech,
  Acanthus mollis 'Latifolius'; 0°
- Monkshood,
  Aconitum carmichaelii 'Wilsonii'; –40°
- Japanese anemone, *Anemone hybrida* 'Honorine Jobert'; –30°
- Goat's beard, *Aruncus dioicus;* –30°
- False indigo, *Baptisia australis;* –40°
- Bugbane, *Cimicifuga japonica;* –30°
- Black snakeroot,
  Cimicifuga racemosa; –40°
- Heartleaf crambe,
  Crambe cordifolia; –10°
- Cardoon, *Cynara cardunculus;* 0°
- Common foxglove,
  Digitalis purpurea; –30°
- Globe thistle,
  Echinops ritro 'Veitch's Blue'; –40°
- Joe Pye weed, *Eupatorium purpureum* 'Atropurpureum'; –30°
- Scented penstemon,
  Penstemon palmeri; –40°
- Royal beard tongue,
  Penstemon spectabilis; 10°
- Russian sage,
  Perovskia atriplicifolia 'Longin'; –20°
- New Zealand flax,
  Phormium tenax hybrids; 20°
- Fingerleaf rodgersia,
  Rodgersia aesculifolia; –20°
- Matilija poppy, *Romneya coulteri;* 15°
- Coneflower,
  Rudbeckia nitida 'Herbstsonne'; –40°
- Forsythia sage, *Salvia madrensis;* 20°

Lamb's ears, named for its oblong, woolly white leaves, grows to 1½ feet tall and spreads freely by surface roots.

Delphinium blossoms enrich the summer garden with cool color while providing nectar to a visiting hummingbird.

- Bog sage, *Salvia uliginosa;* 10°
- Chinese meadow rue, *Thalictrum delavayi;* –20°
- Meadow rue, *Thalictrum rochebrunianum;* –20°

PERENNIALS WITH GRAY OR SILVER LEAVES

Many silver- and gray-leaved plants are lovely in their own right. But they show off best when used to contrast plants that have dark green leaves. They also make appealing companions for plants with bright or pastel flowers. Most are sun-lovers that tolerate drought; the hairs that create the silver or gray appearance on leaves reflect heat, keeping leaves cool while offering protection from the drying effects of wind.

- Yarrow, *Achillea clypeolata;* –30°
- Beach wormwood, *Artemisia stellerana;* –30°
- False dittany, *Ballota pseudodictamnus;* 0°
- Snow-in-summer, *Cerastium tomentosum;* –40°
- Cardoon, *Cynara cardunculus;* 0°
- Dead nettle, *Lamium maculatum* 'Beacon Silver', 'Pink Pewter'; –30°

- Crete dittany, *Origanum dictamnus;* 10°
- Russian sage, *Perovskia atriplicifolia;* –20°
- Bethlehem sage, *Pulmonaria saccharata* 'Janet Fisk'; –30°
- Cobweb houseleek, *Sempervivum arachnoideum;* –20°
- Dusty miller, *Senecio viravira;* 10°
- Lamb's ears, *Stachys byzantina;* –30°
- Woolly thyme, *Thymus pseudolanuginosus;* –20°
- Mullein, *Verbascum olympicum;* –20°

PLANTS THAT ATTRACT HUMMINGBIRDS

Hummingbirds are unique among birds in their dependence on nectar to sustain their high energy level. By including some brightly colored flowers in your landscape, you can easily lure them into view. They prefer tubular or trumpet-shaped flowers. To view hummingbirds easily, place plants that attract them near patios and terraces.

- Texas hummingbird mint, *Agastache cana;* –20°
- Golden columbine, *Aquilegia chrysantha;* –30°

- Western columbine, *Aquilegia formosa;* –30°
- Crocosmia, *Crocosmia* 'Lucifer'; –10°
- Delphinium, *Delphinium belladonna;* –30°
- Candle delphinium, *Delphinium elatum;* –40°
- Alum root, *Heuchera americana;* –30°
- Coral bells, *Heuchera sanguinea;* –40°
- Lion's tail, *Leonotis leonurus;* 30°
- Cardinal flower, *Lobelia cardinalis;* –40°
- Lupine, *Lupinus* hybrids; –20°
- Maltese cross, *Lychnis chalcedonica;* –30°
- Bee balm, *Monarda didyma;* –30°
- Beard tongue, *Penstemon digitalis;* –30°
- Firecracker penstemon, *Penstemon eatonii;* –30°
- Coral fountain, *Russelia equisetiformis;* 25°
- Pineapple sage, *Salvia elegans;* 10°
- Hummingbird sage, *Salvia spathacea;* 20°
- Scarlet hedge nettle, *Stachys coccinea;* 0°
- California fuchsia, *Zauschneria californica (Epilobium canum canum);* 10°

choosing and planting a lawn

It's hard to deny the pleasure of walking barefoot in the grass or playing with the kids on a soft patch of lawn. Grass makes a plane of green that ties plants and architecture together and gives the eye relief from brightly colored flowers.

While growing a lush, green lawn gives you a good feeling of accomplishment, it comes at a price. In some locations, lawn care is both labor intensive and costly. For these reasons, the big, high-maintenance, weed-free lawn is disappearing. But if you're smart about lawn size and shape, as well as location and the type of grass you choose, you can enjoy the pleasures of a lawn and fewer downsides.

lawn design

The number-one adjustment you can make to save time and expense is to cut back on the size of the lawn. Consider, for example, that an average American lawn covers some 6,000 square feet. Drop back to 1,000 square feet and you'll still have ample space for play and some chairs, but you'll reduce time spent mowing by more than 80 percent. Here are some other design tips to reduce mowing time:

■ Lawns with straight or gently curving lines can be mowed more quickly than those with sharp curves and tight corners. Consider a kidney-shaped lawn instead of a rectangle.

■ Don't break the lawn into small patches separated by trees, shrubs, or steppingstones. Instead, group plants on grass-free "islands" with mulch covering the soil.

■ Size grass paths for convenient mowing. For example, using a standard 21-inch mower, you can easily cut a path 36 to 40 inches wide in two passes without leaving a narrow unmowed strip.

■ Install a mowing strip of brick, concrete, or flat stone at the edge of the lawn, level with the soil. Run one edge of the lawn mower on the strip while mowing so blades cut grass and edge in one pass.

choosing grasses

There are only a few basic grass types, so if you're planting the first task is to choose a variety that is well adapted to your region.

All lawn grasses belong to one of two categories: cool-season (northern) or warm-season (southern).

Kentucky bluegrass, fescues, and perennial ryegrass are cool-season grasses. Each has dark green, soft leaves and can take cold winters.

Bermuda, bahia, carpet, zoysia, buffalo, and St. Augustine are the warm-season grasses. Their leaves are somewhat stiffer and are olive or yellow-green. They thrive in heat but spend winters a dormant brown.

Easy maintenance and low water use are advantages of this small lawn. Its soft surface is just large enough for relaxing in the sun.

A CLIMATE MAP FOR LAWNS

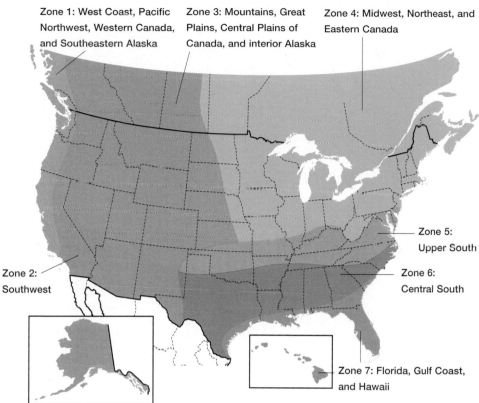

Zone 1: West Coast, Pacific Northwest, Western Canada, and Southeastern Alaska

Zone 3: Mountains, Great Plains, Central Plains of Canada, and interior Alaska

Zone 4: Midwest, Northeast, and Eastern Canada

Zone 2: Southwest

Zone 5: Upper South

Zone 6: Central South

Zone 7: Florida, Gulf Coast, and Hawaii

Zone 3: Mountains, Great Plains, Central Plains of Canada, and interior Alaksa Hot and dry summers, cold winters, and arid. Kentucky bluegrass and fine fescue are most common; native buffalo and blue grama are options throughout the lower states.

Zone 4: Midwest, Northeast, and Eastern Canada Hot and humid summers, cooler near the Great Lakes and coast; very cold winters. Kentucky bluegrass grows best, though it is usually mixed with fine fescue and perennial ryegrass.

Zone 5: Upper South Hot, humid summers and cold winters. Mostly Kentucky bluegrass mixed with fine fescue. Bermuda, tall fescue, and zoysia are options.

Zone 6: Central South Hot and humid summers, relatively mild winters. Bermuda, centipede, tall fescue, and zoysia do well. Use Kentucky bluegrass at higher elevations, St. Augustine in the south.

Zone 7: Florida, Gulf Coast, and Hawaii Summers are hot and humid here, but winters are mild. St. Augustine and zoysia are popular; bahia, bermuda, and centipede are good alternatives.

Named varieties Any lawn grass with a name added to its common grass name is an improved version of the plain grass; for example, 'Galaxy' or 'Glade' Kentucky bluegrass. When you buy seed, check the label and look for specific named varieties of grasses. Check with a nursery or cooperative extension office for varieties recommended for your region.

Climate map Each zone on the map outlines a particular climate for grasses. Find your zone to see which of the grasses will grow best for you.

Zone 1: West Coast, Pacific Northwest, Western Canada, and Southeastern Alaska Cool summers and mild winters; humid. Bent, fine, and tall fescue; Kentucky bluegrass and perennial ryegrass thrive in this region's cool climate.

Zone 2: Southwest Hot summers, relatively mild winters, and arid. Bermuda grows well, as do native buffalo and blue grama. At higher elevations, Kentucky bluegrass and tall fescue are options.

soil preparation

Before going to all the work of planting a lawn, get the soil right, whether you're planting with seed, sod, sprigs, or plugs. It's all the same. In each case, the best-looking, easiest to care for lawn is the one with the best soil beneath it. The basics of soil preparation begin on page 144, but be mindful of the following specific needs for lawns.

Attend first to the obvious, such as clearing out rocks, roots, and debris. Then lay out and measure the planting site. You'll need to know its dimensions now, to plant, but also later to fertilize accurately.

The next step is a soil test. It's the best way to ensure your labor produces good results, and it may also save money. A soil test reveals just how much and which kind of amendment is needed to get the soil right. If amendments are called for, spread them evenly over the soil and till them in. Finally, use a rake to smooth and level the area.

One area in which the method of planting makes a difference is the

The day before laying sod, water soil so that it's moist but not soggy. Unroll the strips and lay sections in a brick-bond fashion, staggering rows. Press edges together firmly.

For a snug fit around obstacles, use a carpet knife or an old kitchen knife to trim sod.

final grade. For instance, when establishing the final grade for sod, keep in mind you'll need to lower the grade by the thickness of the sod itself, usually about ½ inch. Final grade for seed, on the other hand, should be the actual height of the lawn you want.

If you're planting a lawn around a new house, you may need to buy and bring in topsoil. To add 4 inches of topsoil to a 1,000-square-foot area requires about 12 cubic yards, at a cost anywhere from $10 to $25 a yard. For more details, check with

a nursery. If it doesn't carry topsoil, the staff should be able to recommend a reliable source.

Lawns from sod Weather permitting, you can plant a sod lawn in spring, fall, and even summer, though more frequent watering is needed in the heat of summer.

Measure your space carefully and then order about 10 percent more sod than you need to allow for waste. Finish all the ground preparation before delivery day; sod dries out quickly, so minimize the time it sits unplanted. Also, since rolls are heavy, make sure to have them delivered close to where you will use them. The idea is to work fast, moving the sod from pallet to soil in the least possible time.

To lay sod, begin along the straight edge of a walk, or run a string line for an edge to follow.

Try to use whole pieces; cut only when necessary, using a sharp knife. Stagger seams and don't pull or stretch sod into place—it shrinks a bit as it dries out.

Once you completely cover the area with sod, give it a complete soaking. As Roger Cook notes, this helps get the roots in contact with the soil. For extra insurance, rolling is often recommended. Rolling won't

Roll newly laid sod to press its roots into close contact with the soil. Then water frequently—every day during hot weather—until you're sure roots and soil have connected.

level uneven soil, but it will make sure roots are firmly pressed into contact with the soil and eliminate any gaps and air pockets. Rollers, partially filled with water to give them some weight, are available at rental yards for about $15 a day.

Keep the sod moist until roots connect with the underlying soil. Water regularly, which means every day in warm or sunny weather, and continue until you can tug on the sod and feel it resist, indicating it has rooted. Try to minimize foot traffic until the sod is established.

GETTING THE LAWN YOU WANT

Should you choose seed or sod for your new lawn? What about sprigs and plugs?

Seeding is relatively easy and inexpensive: about $40 buys enough seed for 1,000 square feet, and the job of spreading it and nursing it is quite manageable. If you have more than 4,000 square feet, consider hiring a contractor to hydroseed the area. Hydroseeding is a process in which a slurry mixture of grass seed, fibrous material, and water is sprayed through a hose. It's much faster than hand seeding, and you benefit from the experience of the contractors who do the work. But at about $80 per 1,000 square feet, it's also more expensive. Regardless of how a seed-grown lawn is sown, it needs a few months and extra care to sink its roots.

Hydroseeding is an efficient way to sow seed over a large area. It's much faster than sowing seed with a spreader, and much less expensive than sod.

If you need a lawn in a hurry and don't have acres to cover, sod is probably the way to go. At 35 to 50 cents per square foot, sod costs 5 to 10 times more than seed, which makes sense because someone else took the time to raise it from seed.

The type of lawn you choose also affects your decision. You can sow the seed of all cool-season grasses, and most of the warm-season grasses. But some warm-season lawn options are hybrids that don't produce seed and are available only as sod, sprigs, or plugs. Using sprigs or plugs will make sod go further: sprigs are pieces of lawn stems planted like seed; plugs are 2- to 4-inch sections of sod with roots and soil planted one at a time, 1 to 2 feet apart. Neither provides an instant lawn, but both provide substantial cost savings.

lawns from seed

If you're starting a new lawn or restoring a worn-out one, seed is often the most practical choice.

Timing Throughout North America, early fall is the best time to seed a lawn, although exactly when "early fall" occurs shifts according to latitude: from late August in Montana to late September in Nashville. The reason for early fall is simple: the weather then is cool, encouraging grass seeds to germinate instead of weeds. That said, most people sow seed lawns in spring, but for reasons less to do with horticulture than psychology.

Sowing a seed lawn in spring can work just fine, but you'll need to be extra vigilant to get lush grass without lots of weeds. One option is applying the pre-emergent herbicide siduron. It can stop crabgrass and other weeds from germinating without hurting most lawn seeds, but be sure to read the label before using it. Also, hydroseeding offers an extra margin of insurance (see "Getting the lawn you want," on page 179). A protective layer of mulch is part of the sprayed slurry, and the contractor will select a seed mix for fast germination that just might beat out the weeds.

Sowing After selecting and purchasing the seed and preparing the soil,

Once the soil is prepared and graded, scatter seed with a spreader. For a larger lawn, use a walk behind broadcast spreader.

you'll need to disperse the seed evenly over the lawn area. The amount to sow depends on the type of seed: use 2 to 4 pounds of tiny Kentucky bluegrass seeds per 1,000 square feet ($15 to $30 per pound); or 10 pounds of larger perennial ryegrass for the same area ($3 to $6 per pound). If you buy a packaged seed product, seeding rates will be prominent in the label directions, but they are usually conservative and assume good conditions. Especially if spring seeding, sow generously, even to the point of doubling up on the recommended rate. A thick stand

of lawn seed is the best defense against weeds.

For a small lawn, use a hand-held seeder that scatters seed in a circular motion as you walk. If you have a large area to cover, use a walk-behind seeder. Fill the bin with seed, calibrate the openings to the recommended setting, and release the seed by squeezing the handle. Once the seed is on the soil surface, gently pull a leaf rake, tines up, over the surface, to cover the seeds. The idea is to cover the seeds with soil, but very lightly.

A plastic garden rake with tines turned upward works well to cover seed with a bit of soil. The soil will prevent the seed from blowing away or drying out.

one area to another, or set the timer on an irrigation system to water once or twice a day; a light 5- to 10-minute sprinkling to wet the top $\frac{1}{4}$ to $\frac{1}{2}$ inch of soil is all that is needed. Germination times vary from one type of grass to another, but you should see young green blades in one to two weeks.

Spread $\frac{1}{4}$ inch of mulch, then roll to press seeds firmly against soil.

Next, apply a $\frac{1}{4}$-inch layer of mulch atop the surface to help keep the seeds moist and help prevent them from washing away in a rain. Then roll an empty drum roller over the mulched seed to ensure that the seed is pressed firmly against the soil.

Last, water well and, especially, water often. Soaking the soil underneath the seed isn't necessary, but keeping the seed and the top inch or so moist is critical. The seed must not dry out once it has been saturated.

Water after the initial soaking at least once a day. When it is hot, dry, or windy, more frequent watering will be necessary. Keep your local climate in mind: lawns in bonedry Phoenix or Barstow

will need more frequent watering than those in humid Houston or Boston.

The gentle spray of an oscillating or fan-type sprinkler is good for a newly seeded lawn. Move it from

Water the seedbed often enough to keep it moist, at least twice a day in hot and dry weather.

tip: seed labels

Planting a new lawn isn't cheap and it is a lot of work, so it's important to make sure you're buying high-quality seed. Here's what to look for on seed labels.

■ **NAME** The types of grasses should be listed by specific variety name, not a generic name.

■ **GERMINATION PERCENT** There should be at least 75 percent for Kentucky bluegrass and 85 percent for perennials such as ryegrass, fine fescue, and tall fescue.

■ **WEED SEEDS** They're listed as a percentage by weight. Acceptable limits range from 0.3 percent to 0.5 percent.

■ **OTHER CROP SEEDS** Though not weeds, they are off types that can detract from your lawn's quality. Avoid mixes that include more than 1 percent.

■ **INERT MATTER** Avoid any mix that includes more than 5 percent. The lower the percentage, the better the seed mix.

Dethatching machines have spinning, knife-like blades that cut into the soil and in the process pull up excess thatch. A layer of more than ¾ inch will prevent germinating seeds from taking hold.

reseeding a worn-out lawn

If at least half of your lawn still looks okay, it probably makes more sense to overseed it than to totally remove it and start over. The process is basically the same as for a new lawn, but some steps are adjusted to allow for seeding into an existing lawn rather than onto bare soil.

There are many reasons that a lawn may weaken over time, some obvious and others less so. Before you reseed, consider the causes of the existing lawn's decline. Too little water and fertilizer and too low or too high pH are common causes. A soil test is the only way to know

for sure whether the problem is with the soil's pH, fertility, or both. If soil conditions are the cause, be sure to correct them before replanting. If trees are shrouding the lawn in shade, prune them so more light can reach the grass.

Preparing Ideal reseeding time— early fall—is the same as for seeding a new lawn. If perennial weeds have overwhelmed the lawn, consider spraying first with a nonselective herbicide, such as one containing glyphosate, to kill the existing lawn and weeds. It's not essential, especially if you're not aiming for a perfect lawn. But spraying will reduce the

number of weeds that compete with the grass seeds. If you spray, do it during a period of active growth. Then wait for the weeds and lawn to die, about 10 to 14 days.

The next step is to remove as much of the old lawn as possible by cutting it very short. After mowing and removing all the clippings, go over the lawn with a dethatching machine. Also called a vertical mower, it has spinning blades that slice down through the lawn and slightly into the soil, chopping and pulling up old lawn and weeds and slightly cultivating the soil; you can rent a machine for about $100 a day. Rake up and either compost or dispose of the loose debris.

If your soil is compacted, aerate it after dethatching. The most effective tool is a gas-powered aerating machine. It pulls out little plugs of soil, leaving holes that relieve compaction and create hundreds of openings for seeds, water, and air. You can rent an aerator at most tool-rental companies for about $60 a day.

To smooth out a bumpy lawn and to make certain that seed and soil make good contact, cover the dethatched and aerated lawn with a ½-inch layer of compost mixed with screened topsoil. Spread it with a

An aerating machine opens small holes in lawns by pulling out cores of soil.

rake to fill any low spots. Also add any amendments or fertilizers that a soil test indicates are needed.

Sow seeds Hand-cast seed over small areas using broad sweeping motions, or use a spreader for a larger area. To ensure even coverage, divide the total amount of seed in half and spread one half walking in one direction and the other half walking the other way. Since seed is cheap (relative to the cost of your time and labor), double the recommended amount the label states for a given area.

Settle seeds Pass over the seeded area with the back of a leaf rake to settle the seeds into the soil and slightly cover them. Next, firm seed into the soil using a drum roller.

Water Finally and most importantly, water. Just as for a newly seeded lawn (page 181), it's critical to keep the seeds moist until roots set into the soil. Gradually increase the amount of water and the time between waterings to encourage the roots to grow downward.

Mow Do not rush to mow your new grass; wait until it is at least 3 inches tall before cutting it, and then cut it back to 2 inches high. Be sure to use a bagging attachment so clippings are picked up and not left to smother young plants. Once grass matures, you can leave the clippings in place.

A rotary spreader scatters seed fast over a large area. Sow seed when the forecast calls for mild weather, and double the seeding rate the package recommends.

PATCHING A LAWN

If only a small section of your lawn has deteriorated enough to require replanting, follow the same procedure described for complete renovation. But rather than rent lots of equipment, you can use simpler hand tools, such as a dethatching rake and a hand-aerating tool.

Cut into the lawn around the damaged area with a spade, slicing out a curved line so the repair will blend in better. Remove any clumps of sickly sod, cultivate and amend the soil, and rake it smooth; the surface should be about ½ inch below grade if you're replanting sod, or at grade if sowing seed.

Measure the space and order the amount of sod you need, plus a little extra, or buy the needed amount of seed. Lay the new sod, cutting as needed to fit, or sow seed, gently rake it in, and mulch. Whether you use sod or seed, water frequently until new growth is well underway.

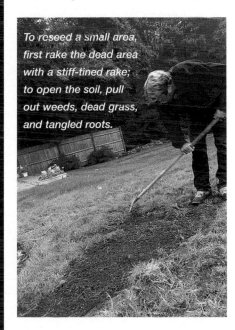

To reseed a small area, first rake the dead area with a stiff-tined rake; to open the soil, pull out weeds, dead grass, and tangled roots.

resource directory

cooperative extension

Each state's land-grant university includes a cooperative extension program that provides information, publications, and sometimes soil testing. Remote offices are located in each county. Check in your telephone directory under the university name. For links to cooperative extension web sites, see: www.ext.colostate.edu/links/linkexte.html. Ohio State University sponsors a search engine that includes plant-related guides from 46 different universities and government institutions across the U.S. and Canada. See http://plantfacts.osu.edu/web.

soil testing

Appropriate Technology Transfer for Rural Areas (ATTRA)
Fayetteville, AR
800-346-9140
http://attra.ncat.org/attra-pub/soil-lab.html
Links to soil-testing services and kits

Midwest Laboratories
Omaha, NE
402-334-7770
www.midwestlabs.com

Soil and Plant Lab
Santa Clara, CA
408-727-0330
www.soilandplantlaboratory.com

University of Massachusetts Soil Testing Lab
Amherst, MA
413-545-2311
www.umass.edu/plsoils/soiltest

Wallace Laboratories
El Segundo, CA
310-615-0116
www.bettersoils.com

Woods End Research Laboratory
Mt. Vernon, ME
207-293-2457
www.woodsend.org

poisonous plants

Poisons and toxins are common in many plants, that use them as a means of self-defense. See the Cornell University Poisonous Plants Informational Database at www.ansci.cornell.edu/plants/index.html.

design-related web sites

Planning the Home Landscape, by William C. Welch, Extension Landscape Horticulturist, Texas A&M University, http://aggie-horticulture.tamu.edu/extension/homelandscape/home.html

Residential Landscape Design, by David Williams, Extension Horticulturist, Assistant Professor, and Ken Tilt, Extension Horticulturist, Associate Professor, both in Horticulture at Auburn University; www.aces.edu/department/-extcomm/publications/anr/ANR-0813/anr813.html

Residential Landscaping, by M.A. Powell, Specialist in Charge, Horticulture Extension, North Carolina Cooperative Extension Service, North Carolina State University; http://ipm.ncsu.edu/urban/horticulture/res_landscaping.html

associations and organizations

American Society of Landscape Architects
Washington, DC
202-898-2444
www.asla.org

American Wood Preservers Association
Granbury, TX
817-326-6300
www.awpa.com

American Wood Preservers Institute
Fairfax, VA
703-204-0500
www.awpi.org

Associated Landscape Contractors of America
Herndon, VA
703-736-9666
www.alca.org

Association of Professional Landscape Designers
Chicago, IL
312-201-0101
www.apld.com

Brick Industry Association
Reston, VA
703-620-0010
www.bia.org

California Redwood Association
Novato, CA
888-225-7339
www.calredwood.org

Forest Products Laboratory
Madison, WI
608-231-9200
www.fpl.fs.fed.us

information about working with and caring for wood

Forest Stewardship Council
www.fscus.org
Information about certified forest products; includes a link to a searchable database of products by type or wood species

Interlocking Concrete Pavement Institute
Washington, DC
202-712-9036
www.icpi.org

The Irrigation Association
Falls Church, VA
703-536-7080
www.irrigation.org

National Concrete Masonry Association
Herndon, VA
703-713-1900
www.ncma.org/use/srw.html

Plastic Lumber Trade Association
Akron, OH
330-762-1963
www.plasticlumber.org

alternative deck materials

Boardwalk Composite Lumber
CertainTeed Corp.
800-782-8777
www.compositedecking.com

ChoiceDek
AERT, Inc.
800-951-5117
www.choicedek.com

Nexwood
Composite Technology Resources Ltd.
888-763-9966
www.nexwood.com

Trex Company LLC
800-289-8739
www.trex.com

U.S. Plastic Lumber Company
800-653-2784
www.oikos.com

deck & patio furnishings

Gardener's Eden
800-822-9600
www.gardenerseden.com

Gardener's Supply Company
800-863-1700
www.gardeners.com

Kinsman Company
800-733-4146
www.kinsmangarden.com

Plow & Hearth
800-627-1712
www.plowhearth.com

Smith & Hawken
800-940-1170
www.smithandhawken.com

playground equipment

Childlife
Holliston, MA
508-429-4639
www.childlife.com

Creative Playthings
800-247-9464
www.creativeplaythings.com

Fibar Systems
Armonk, NY
800-342-2721
www.fibar.com
Shredded, engineered wood fiber
for play surfaces

Play Systems Inc.
Marietta, GA
800-445-7529
www.playset.com

Rainbow Play Systems, Inc.
800-724-6269
www.rainbowplay.com

irrigation suppliers

Agrifim
Fresno, CA
559-431-2003
www.agrifim.com
Drip irrigation supplies

Buckner By Storm
Fresno, CA
800-328-4469
www.bucknerirrigation.com
Sprinklers, valves, and other irrigation
supplies

Hunter Industries, Inc.
www.hunterindustries.com
Rotary and spray sprinklers, controllers,
and sensors

Netafim
Fresno, CA
559-453-6800
www.netafimusa.com
Drip irrigation supplies

Rainbird
800-724-6247
www.rainbird.com
Wide variety of irrigation supplies

Toro
800-367-8676
www.toro.com/irrigation/allirrigation.html
Wide variety of irrigation supplies

The Urban Farmer Store
San Francisco, CA
415-661-2204

www.urbanfarmerstore.com
Retail dealer of professional irrigation, outdoor lighting, and pond equipment

landscape edging

The Curbing Edge
877-955-3343
www.curbingedge.com

DuraEdge
www.jdrussellco.com/DURAEDGE/
duraedge.htm
Steel landscape edging

Kwik Kerb
www.kwikkerb.org
321-257-2002

Oly-Ola Sales Inc.
Villa Park, IL
800-334-4647
www.olyola.com

outdoor lighting

Cooper Lighting
www.cooperlighting.com/brands/
lumiere

Focus Industries Landscape Lighting
888-882-1350
www.focusindustries.com

FX Luminaire
800-688-1269
www.fxl.com

Hadco
717-359-7131
www.hadcolighting.com

Intermatic, Inc.
815-675-7000
www.intermatic.com

Kim Lighting
626-968-5666
www.kimlighting.com

Nightscaping
800-544-4840
www.nightscaping.com

Unique Lighting Systems
800-955-4831
www.uniquelighting.com

retaining walls

Ideal Concrete Block
Westford, MA
781-894-3200
www.idealconcreteblock.com

Keystone Retaining Wall Systems
Minneapolis, MN
800-891-8791
www.keystonewalls.com

Lock+Load Retaining Wall Systems
877-901-9998
www.lock-load.com

RisiStone Retaining Wall Systems
800-626-9255
www.risistone.com

Westcon Pavers & Retaining Walls
Olympia, WA
877-837-8904
www.westconpavers.com

landscape tools & supplies

A.M. Leonard, Inc.
Piqua, OH
800-543-8955
www.amleo.com

Gempler's
Belleville, WI
800-382-8473
www.gemplers.com

Lee Valley Tools
Ogdensburg, NY
800-871-8158
www.leevalley.com

Peaceful Valley Farm Supply
Grass Valley, CA
888-784-1722
www.groworganic.com

landscape plants

Carroll Gardens
Westminster, MD
800-638-6334
www.carrollgardens.com

Forestfarm
Williams, OR
541-846-7269
www.forestfarm.com

Gossler Farms Nursery
Springfield, OR
541-746-3922

Greer Gardens
Eugene, OR
800-548-0111
www.greergardens.com

High Country Gardens
Santa Fe, NM
800-925-9387
www.highcountrygardens.com

Mellinger's
North Lima, OH
800-321-7444
www.mellingers.com

Musser Forests, Inc.
Indiana, PA
800-643-8319
www.musserforests.com

Roslyn Nursery
Dix Hills, NY
631-643-9347
www.roslynnursery.com

Wayside Gardens
Hodges, SC
800-845-1124
www.waysidegardens.com

White Flower Farm
Litchfield, CT
800-503-9624
www.whiteflowerfarm.com

lawn information

Colorado State University Turf Program
http://csuturf.colostate.edu

The National Turfgrass Evaluation Program
www.ntep.org/contents2.shtml
Evaluates turfgrass varieties and publishes results

Ohio State University
http://ohioline.osu.edu/lines/lawns.html

Penn State Agricultural Sciences
www.agronomy.psu.edu/Extension/Turf/Diagnose.html#Mowing

Purdue Turfgrass Program
www.agry.purdue.edu/turf

Texas A&M University Turfgrass
http://aggieturf.tamu.edu

Turfgrass Information Center
Michigan State University
www.lib.msu.edu/tgif

Turfgrass Producers International
www.turfgrasssod.org/links.html

lawn seeds

Ampac Seed Co.
541-928-1651
www.ampacseed.com

Bailey Seed
800-407-7713
www.outsidepride.com

Budd Seed, Inc.
www.turf.com

Lawngrass.com
www.lawngrass.com

Murff Turf Farms Inc.
800-892-6704
www.murffturf.com

Outsidepride.com
877-255-8470
www.outsidepride.com

Pennington Seed Inc.
800-285-7333
www.penningtonseed.com

Seedland
386-963-2080
www.seedland.com

Seed Superstore
866-634-0001
www.seedsuperstore.com

Summit Seed Inc.
815-468-7333
www.summitseed.com

Turf-Seed Inc.
800-247-6910
www.turf-seed.com

credits

index

Page numbers in **boldface** refer to photographs and illustrations.